A MAN WITH A HAT
— collected stories and prose —

JOHN McNAMEE

Weaver Publications

Published by Weaver Publications, 19F Nicholas Street, Dublin 8.

First published in the Republic of Ireland 2005

ISBN 0-9513044-6-1

Editorial assistance by James McAuley and Joseph Woods
Cover illustration by Pablo Galiano
Layout by Oldtown
Printed by Colorman Ireland Ltd

Some of these stories and articles have appeared previously in the
following: RTÉ Radio 1, *The Irish Times, The Examiner, The Irish
Press, Evening Press, Big Issues Magazine, Sunday Business Post,
North-East News, Reality Magazine, Northside People, Evening News.*

This book is dedicated to Eileen, Patricia, Elizabeth, Peter, Conor Senior and Junior, Carly, Patricia, Richard, Derek, Jeffrey, Amelia, Edel, Stephanie, Charlie, Jack, Adrian, Lorna, Simon, Paddy, Lucy, Patricia the younger, James, Betty and Hugh and all the gang – a family of hope.

" "

"Nelson Mandela, a gem of a fella"

– Damien Dempsey

INNOCENCE

They laughed at one I loved –
The triangular hull that hung
Under the Big Forth. They said
That I was bounded by the whitethorn hedges
Of the little farm and did not know the world.
But I knew that love's doorway to life
Is the same doorway everywhere.

– Patrick Kavanagh

"It is still only an Irishman who can cry for the polluted blood of humanity"

– John Steinbeck, from *East of Eden*

"If you never get into trouble, you'll never know how to get out of it."

–Sage wisdom imparted to the author while he was under severe duress, financial, spiritual and romantic, by a Dublin taxi driver which had been told to him by his own father. In transit late at night in Dublin city.

"Spes ancora vitae est"
Hope is the anchor of life

– Family motto

CONTENTS

Writing and Writers

INTRODUCTION

"My figures seem disposed to stagnate without crowds around them," wrote Baudelaire, who desperately needed to walk the streets for inspiration for his work.

Dublin's northside provides a Bauedelairean magic lantern for her poets. Here, Joyce hovered in expectation of an epiphany, and James Stephens and Austin Clarke also bathed in the rose glow of the Victorian streets, set off by the harmony of massive Georgian squares against a backdrop of blue hills, set above the largest and most beautiful park in any capital city.

John McNamee has his finger on the pulse of this northside culture, which is different from Rathmines, Rathgar, Ranelagh and Rathfarnham, as Greenwich Village is from Brooklyn Heights. He took to the Dublin habit of strolling, and spent his free time on the streets, sniffing the air and letting the pictures in his mind become part of him. His background was lower middle class. The family had a Sunday roast. He would meet his mother for lunch at the Monument Creamery. As a boy, he wanted to acquire a raven like Cuchulainn. Everything on the landscape meant something different to him:

> "The sun reappeared at intervals with a bright glow when the clouds drifting by were not too dense to stop it penetrating the leaden atmosphere. In the background, a lone small red bloom clung bravely to the stem of a fragile role tree which was tossed about in the brisk breeze."

Like Wilde's *Happy Prince,* he would watch out for the sight of the first swallows and the arrival of the swans on the Royal Canal, between Cross Guns' Bridge and Binn's Bridge. He was a useful centre-half on a well-known northside Schoolboys Soccer team. In *The Trophy* he has told of how he once pawned the Perpetual Challenge Cup and found himself in a dilemma not unlike that in Joyce's story *Araby*.

John McNamee's roots are in the Beat poets. He visited San Francisco in his twenties, as an earlier generation might have made a pilgrimage to Lough Derg. There he learnt how to expand the spirit and dismantle areas of his mind that were unproductive. Rimbaud called this process *dereglement des sens,* and many have made forays into the area without coming out with much to show. But John has managed to hold the fort and emerge with a prose style, and a pad in which to ply his trade. He has written four books of poetry, and this book of short stories and essays is his third in that form. He catches the loneliness of the outcast without overdoing the whine, and occasionally gives us glimpses of those sheer cliffs to which Hopkins horrifyingly hung on.

John McNamee is what the French call *un ecrivain.* This translates as 'a writer' but has different connotations from most of the rubbish now emerging in novels, plays or verse. Here is how he sees his vocation:

> "The canopy of all art is life, what happens in the tent of the artist's creation is his own affair. But writers provide with their camels the means for the world to cross its deserts."

He views the journey in simple terms, though not necessarily easy ones:

> "Indeed how can we know, or have any chance of knowing, unless, like the sunrise and the sunset, we need as a rehearsal a little death and resurrection every day of our lives."

John McNamee has been there and come back to tell us the news. He has got the run of himself, and the poetry programme which he runs for the Bank of Ireland is easily the best poetic venue in Ireland today. Curiously enough, this Beat guy is a real cute organiser. Bully for the bank!

Ulick O'Connor

DUBLIN – CITY OF DREAMS AND NIGHTMARES

AS I LOOK across the street from the all-night café where I pen these lines, at the corner of Aston Quay and Westmoreland Street, a vivid memory is stirred in my mind. It is of a sixteen-year-old student from St Vincent's Christian Brothers in Glasnevin trying to write poetry.

With pen and paper in my hand, I was standing at the north corner of O'Connell Bridge, adjacent to the old Corinthian Cinema. I was trying to describe in verse the skeletal structure of Liberty Hall, then in its girdered cradle of construction.

At the rear of a fish-and-chip shop opposite the old Abbey Theatre, I and my fellow Sunday afternoon visitors to the Corinthian (or the Ranch as it was affectionately known, because it generally showed cowboy pictures) purchased a greasy vinegar-soaked culinary offering called a potato burger or some such euphemism. It was devoured just as ravenously as if it had been a loaf of bread in famine-stricken Somalia.

Just beyond the lights of Butt Bridge, which were barely visible in the early morning darkness, was all the glory of the international navies which paid and still pay courtesy visits to our capital city. French cigarettes were provided generously by sailors seeking information in pidgin English about the venues of dances and the general whereabouts of Dublin girls.

Across O'Connell Bridge on the east side of O'Connell Street, facing the Metropole, was the Broadway Café – scene of chatting-up over innumerable cups of coffee, or if finances permitted, a Knickerbocker Glory or a Banana Split. But the ice-cream was usually provided by an elder brother for my younger sister and myself in the Broadway on a Sunday morning after Mass. Before the Sunday roast in Glasnevin, my sister, being the pet, would succeed in getting a lift home on the back of the brother's scooter, which were then all the rage. Afterwards the bubble cars had their burst of short-lived glory, like an army of mayflies.

On D'Olier Street was an advertising agency where I had a summer job as an office boy with the princely salary of £2.10s.0d. a week. I think I got the job because I corrected the elderly gentleman who was conducting the interview about the exact location of Elvery's Sports Shop, known as the Elephant House. This was situated at the corner of O'Connell Street and Middle Abbey Street, where there is now a fast-food restaurant.

On the Sunday mornings of my youth a bus at Burgh Quay took a group of us Boy Scouts to Enniskerry to walk the three miles to Glencree. We would climb Maulin Mountain, after cooking lunch over a camp fire, then we would walk back to Enniskerry through Powerscourt and sing songs on the bus on the way home.

Also on Burgh Quay was the first job I ever had in my life, in a Wimpey Bar making Wimpies, which in their own way were the foretaste of McDonalds. Opposite the Broadway Café on O'Connell Street was the fabled Metropole, with the best toasted sandwiches in the world, complete with cinema and ballroom where so many sisters met their husbands.

Caffolla's, on O'Connell Street, was where I spent my Confirmation money on a high tea of egg and chips. Parnell Square was where I worked briefly in Dublin County Council as a temporary clerical officer, while still trying to write poetry. The Gate Theatre was where I saw for the first time *Waiting for Godot*, a production by the UCD Drama Soc. The Municipal Gallery was where I saw my first Renoir.

The Ambassador Cinema on Parnell Square was where I saw Paul Newman and Jackie Gleeson in *The Hustler*. The entrance fee was acquired thanks to a mythical back molar tooth which had to be extracted in the Dental Hospital in Lincoln Place. I pocketed the fee of five shillings. Also on Parnell Square is the Rotunda Hospital where I was born in 1947, remembered in folklore memory as the freezing winter of 1947.

On O'Connell Street next door to the Carlton Cinema, at the Monument Creamery (famous for its soda bread) on a Saturday after school, I would meet my mother for lunch, since the family treasury was still solvent, as my father had been paid the previous day.

Down the street, around the corner on Henry Street, next door to the old Radio Éireann studios, was Hafners, home of the legendary sausages and white pudding with the potent seasoning. They made up a luxurious fry on Sunday mornings with potato bread from the Country Shop. The cup of tea that kept it company was in a league all of its own.

The father of a school friend of mine worked as a scenic designer backstage at the Royal Theatre, next door to the Regal Cinema in Hawkins Street. We had a sympathetic teacher (he's still teaching in the same school), who would let us off early to use our complimentary tickets to see Tommy Dando on the organ, Jack Cruise and the leggy Royalettes.

Sunday morning visits to the Bird Market, situated in the shadow of St Patrick's Cathedral, were also indulged in. My ambition was to acquire a raven, my mind being full of the heroic imagery of Cúchulainn.

I made, what seemed to me as a child, the impossible climb to the wire-netted summit of Dublin's one-time leading landmark, Nelson's Pillar, a monument to a once-honoured father of the British Empire, with his one eye and missing arm. This vantage point provided a unique view of the rooftops, spires and chimneys of my native city. The television series *The Fugitive* with David Janson, the luckless doctor in search of a one-armed man who could clear his name and end his misfortune as a hunted criminal, was extremely popular on the new television station at the time. Some Dublin wit recorded, soon after Nelson was blown up, that they had got the one-armed man at last.

The emergence of the coffee shops like the New Amsterdam in Duke Street was Dublin's delayed response to the Beatnik movement which germinated in Montparnasse and Greenwich Village. The Dublin criteria for being a fully-fledged Beatnik was to wear a long black sweater down to your arse, unkempt beard, jeans and sandals. The same pre-requisites existed for lady Beatniks, but the beard was not compulsory.

According to Aldous Huxley who visited Dublin, "If there is nothing left to be said in conversation, it is a Dubliner who'd say it." Also, "According to its citizens, Dublin is the greatest metropolis in Christendom."

John Mitchell, author of *The Jail Journal*, heading out of Dublin Bay on his way to Van Diemen's Land, wrote, "Dublin, city of genteel dastards and bellowing slaves."

Dublin today could be described as having more wind-up merchants than there are clock-tuners in Switzerland.

The folk scene arrived in Dublin with the immensely popular Saturday night concerts in what was once the old Grafton Cinema. The yo-yo came and went, as did the hula-hoop with some Bengal lancers making a fortune.

The Prince's Bar was demolished by the same killer blow that lowered the Capitol Theatre. Tommy Rogers was the last manager. There was a famous busker of his time whose terrain included the Sunday afternoon matinee queue for the Adelphi Cinema. Among the most famous numbers from his extensive repertoire were "The Day that Mexico Gave Up the Rumba to Do the Rock and Roll" and "South of the Border Down Mexico Way." In those days buskers performed without musical accompaniment. Then came The Beatles and The Rolling Stones which changed a lot of things for a lot of people.

For me, the clearest view of Dublin is through the lens of returning to it from abroad. On returning to Dublin by plane or ship like so many before you, you think that this time, maybe this time you will stay and settle snugly into her arms, but reality is different, very different.

BROTHER AND SISTER

AT 3.15pm, the postman walked the length of the road, along one side of which ran a railway goods line and beyond this, the Royal Canal, where in summertime some of the youth of north Dublin went swimming. His peaked hat, tilted slightly, gave his face an almost aggressive look, but he was just a bit gruff rather than aggressive.

It was the end of November and the weather forecast after the news predicted snow. The foreboding presence of Mountjoy Jail opposite number 47 gave the cold weather something to feel brutal about. The lady of the house poured some milk into the cat's bowl. "Now Smokey there's a good kitten. Come and get your milk." Mrs Murray looked at the clock in the kitchen. She was expecting a letter from her sister in Co Monaghan, which she hoped would contain news that the turkey and Christmas cake would arrive for the festive season.

At 3.30pm the postman's knock could be heard at the front door. Mrs Murray left her baking to one side in the pantry. She gaily hummed her way down the tiled hall and wiped the flour off her hands on her floral patterned apron as she went. The letter contained word that the turkey was ready and would come later with the cake from Madge Aherne's bakery. In the backyard Tim, the mongrel dog, chewed on the remains of the dinner. The next knock on the door would be one of the youngest children arriving home from school.

Aileen was the first of the children to arrive in from the cold. "You must be famished," said Mrs Murray at the front door. "Would you like a cup of tea?" "Yes," came the reply. "But first let me go upstairs and change my uniform."

Mrs Murray watched out the window with the view of the back garden as the water flowed from the tap into the kettle. The sun hung low in the grey cloudy sky. It reappeared at intervals with a bright glow when the clouds drifting by were not too dense to stop it penetrating the leaden atmosphere. In the background, a lone small red bloom clung bravely to the stem of a fragile rose tree which was tossed about in the brisk breeze. She thought about her son in Canada whom she never heard from. How was he? He never wrote home at all. She thought also about her husband. He was the one who made her sad while her children made her happy. He would probably be in the pub until closing time. He was a handsome man in his mid-forties, with a fondness for the jar which caused her much anguish and many novenas. Perhaps she could get him to go to AA again.

While Aileen, the nine-year-old, was upstairs changing her clothes another knock came to the door. That would be Paul, thought Mrs Murray, as she again made her way down the tiled hall. He could see his mother was glad to see him. He was no sooner through the door when he asked permission to let the dog into the house.

Tim could hear and recognise the boy's footsteps walking down the hall. This made him euphoric. He scratched furiously at the back door. On opening it the animal jumped up at Paul and proceeded to make sounds of friendship while wagging the rear of his body vigorously with its docked tail.

"Hello Tim," said the boy. This made the animal even

more excited.

"Mammy, can I go down to Phillipa's house?" asked Aileen on coming into the kitchen.

"Come and get this cup of tea and get yourself warmed up before you go down there," was the reply.

Aileen's black hair and dark looks had won her many bars of chocolate from an Italian gentleman who had been staying in the house. He was reminded so much of Italian children that he wanted to express his homesickness in some way.

"Oh goody, Mammy, you're cooking an apple cake," said the little girl.

"You should've made mince pies," said Paul.

"You're always the same. Never satisfied," said his mother.

"Can I have a biscuit with my cup of tea?" asked Paul.

"Oh, I suppose you can," she relented. "But God help the woman that gets you. How come Aileen doesn't ask for a biscuit?"

"I need more food than she does because I am a boy." Aileen stood with arms akimbo, a big grin on her face, delighted at the points of one-upmanship she had won over her brother.

The two, brother and sister, sat facing each other across the kitchen table with cups of tea and biscuits between them. Finally Paul could stand the silence of defeat no longer and with a slight movement of his feet tapped Aileen's under the table, and muttered from behind clenched teeth:

"I want my rubber back and that little Lulu comic you took out of my room last night."

"They're mine now," she replied. Then she cried out in a strident voice, "Mammy, Paul kicked me."

Mrs Murray came dashing into the kitchen from her pantry. "Paul go out and play," she commanded. Paul slowly got up from his chair and with downcast eyes made his way towards the door. Now there was no chance of getting money for sweets. It was pointless to ask.

Teatime came around and Aileen and Paul faced each other across the tea table. Paul hissed at his sister, "I want my rubber and comic back." Aileen said nothing as her father might walk in. She definitely did not want to be on the wrong side of her father's humour. Maura, the fourteen-year-old sister to Paul and Aileen brought in the food. It was fish – not their favourite. They were both unhappy about the bones.

It had become colder and both brother and sister hoped very much that it would snow. At 7.00pm Mrs Murray put on her tweed winter coat in the hall and combed her hair in the mirror. The grey hairs did not bother her anymore. She felt they gave her more character. As her ageing hands, the result of much toil, gripped the door knob, her two children made their way upstairs to their bedrooms.

"Be good while I'm at church," she called from the door.

She prayed at the church for her children, the son in Canada whom she never heard from, her husband and the Pope's intentions.

Paul, looking out from his window, could see the light in the cells in Mountjoy. Whenever he did anything wrong his mother told him that's where he would end up. This made him look at the dull grey building very quizzically. As he watched, it began snowing quite heavily, like some vast yawn spilling from the heavens. With this fall of snow there would be ice on the canal. Slides would form on city streets allow-ing easy passage through space, and sometimes a fall and a cut knuckle. Bad cess to it anyway. The soccer matches would take place on a field of snow white, white for the truth of all the murk lying beneath the green stagnant surface of Dublin's Liffey and watery soul. The white manna from heaven, settling on all kinds of hidden crevices that hitherto stood gaping, like bad teeth in the need of filling, where the shame of poverty with its spiritual pain would be silenced by people experiencing Christian love for birds, and creatures of the countryside pecking at the dry bone of nature.

The magic of the night in November where the moon hung high like a chandelier, the light bulbs of stars flickering and winking the thoughts of the saints, to the few people looking upwards through the shaft of light of a city street lamp and falling snow. Paul got out of bed and saw millions of white flakes. His excitement overcame the coldness of his feet. He went into Aileen's room.

"It's going to stick to the ground," he cried. Suddenly they heard the pleading sound of a kitten's voice coming from somewhere near the front gate of the house. It was not Smokey's cry because they could distinguish that from other cats.

She asked him to rescue the animal. Paul put on his overcoat and made his way down the stairs hoping against hope that he would not disturb Maura who was trying to concentrate on her homework while listening to Radio Luxembourg. Paul carefully and noiselessly opened the front door. Making his way down the front path he was met with a cold blast of wind. He found the white kitten sheltering under the left front wheel of a car. He carefully placed the furry creature inside the breast of his coat. Fortunately

Maura did not hear any of his coming and going. When he got back upstairs it was plain that the kitten would sleep in his bed. Tomorrow would bring trouble. The last sound he heard before going to sleep was the white kitten purring happily beside him.

In the pub the little bit of electricity that the whiskey had instilled in Mister Murray's bloodstream made the conversation with the brothers Maguire more enjoyable than an evening at home flutterin' around the house and the endless insecurity of it all. With a sigh he said to himself, "Tomorrow's another day – uncertain and unpredictable."

THE SWAN'S EGGS

I KNEW LIAM since we attended Junior Infants in the local convent school. He stood out from the other boys with his wild bunch of brown curly hair, and roguish impish grin. He was wild in his ways but bright in school.

It was when we both left the diligent care of the nuns for the rigorous discipline of the Brothers up the road, that we both began to do some exploring together, in summer, after school when there was plenty of daylight available to get into mischief.

During the year there had been some memorable moments: Hallowe'en, when the straw-filled dummy, for which we were collecting funds, had stopped several buses on the Whitworth Road: the bus drivers, in the fog and poor visibility, had mistaken it for a dead body.

There was also the black thread connected to two knockers on opposite sides of Claude Road, that gave rise to lively chases up back lanes and over garden walls.

While we were both in fifth class in the Christian Brothers, Liam introduced me to the vast expanse of his wild back garden. It was complete with a rabbit hutch and birds' nests. It even contained a monkey tree, and he cared for a number of young pigeons. As far as I was concerned he was a kind of suburban Tarzan, Lord of the Jungle.

On occasion Liam visited my territory after school or on Saturday mornings when we were free. I introduced him to my trees and wilderness at the rear of the Drumcondra Hospital, where we did a lot of climbing, discovering birds' nests and relieving some neighbours of over-ripe gooseberries, apples, cherries and loganberries. The graveyard at the rear of the hospital was as great a mystery for us as the Amazon Basin might be for Jacques Cousteau. It contained vaults and coffins with doors that creaked like Count Dracula's castle and frightened us just as much.

Another favourite rendezvous for adventure was the Botanic Gardens, or the Botts as it was nicknamed. The rambling old house that Liam lived in was situated nearby. So the nooks and crannies of the National Gardens were not unknown to him. He was also well-known to the caretaker, groundsmen and staff. He had a jovial familiar way that made him a popular figure.

The best time for exploration in the Botts was about April or May, when nature's bird and plant life was surging with new energy. Liam had all the right credentials to share in the magical secrets of this sanctuary for active mischief-making boys. One of the favourite activities was to gaze long and deep into the river Tolka which flowed through the green belted banks and entered the ocean at Fairview. We would try and sight an occasional fish in the water.

This summer in question, one of the major spectacles on view for several weeks was a wasps' nest. From a safe distance it was studied, scrutinised and talked about. Later in the afternoon Liam laid bare all the treasures of his birds' eggs collection which was considerable. Every variety from gull to magpie to chaffinch and robin, it even contained a wren's egg. Somehow the idea germinated in our minds about adding a swan's egg to our respective collections.

In the play fields nearby, over the wall and adjacent to the primary school, some of the senior school athletes were preparing for the forthcoming student games. The classrooms were hot and stuffy, even with the windows open and some cool air blowing into the room. The subject was Irish, Mr Rafferty's favourite subject. He was a man with a thick Cork accent and his tongue wrapped itself around the vowels with great gusto. He emitted little spits from his mouth at intervals with the same enthusiasm that one of his students might reserve for devouring bulls-eyes or dolly mixtures. The cadences and rhythms of "Eamonn an Chnoic" were lost on his students who, like Liam and me, were preoccupied with the hand of the clock approaching four. The roomful of thirty-five boys was mentally ready to break from their stalls like a bunch of racehorses just awaiting the starter's white flag on Derby day.

"How much 'ecker' did we get in arithmetic for Brother Delaney tomorrow?" asked Liam, as he put more straw in the white rabbit's hutch with all the smelly pellets of rabbit's droppings.

"There are some fractions and simple interest," I told him, getting a good gawk at the rabbits chewing enthusiastically on the lettuce in the hutch, "but they don't have to be in until first class on Monday morning."

We knew where the swans were nesting on the Royal Canal at Cross Guns Bridge. We were carried on by our tide of enthusiasm to add such a prize to our hoard.

After some reconnaissance of the swan's nest we elected tea-time as the best time to execute our dark deed, that being a time when few people were in the vicinity of the bridge or walking along the canal.

It was arranged that we would meet at the Iona garage across the bridge from the snooker hall and the location of the swan's nest. Innumerable butterflies flapped wildly in my tummy as the excitement and the tension mounted with each step I took towards the bridge.

Some traffic passed over the bridge as we two young bandits with robbery lurking deep in our hearts approached the venue of our show-down with the royal birds of the canal. It was pre-arranged that I would chase the mother swan from the nest of reeds by the canal bank and allow Liam a clearway to pluck two eggs hurriedly from the nest, and escape with haste over the bridge and down the Whitworth Road.

We were both sweating a little in fear and anxiety as we surveyed the road by the canal. The way was clear, the door of the snooker hall open, but it was quiet within and there would be no witnesses. We had reached the point of no return. The thought that we might get caught passed through our minds: the police, court, judge, family shame, embarrassment and disgrace.

The cob was gliding serenely further down the canal towards the lock, unaware of the imminent danger. If we moved quickly, he would not have time to return to the nest and interfere. Liam and I had been told that a swan could break your back with the strength of one of their wings. I had a stick to chase the mother swan from the nest; my heart was beating wildly in its rib cage in fear and excitement.

The hen rose angrily from her nest to full stature as I approached with the stick, like St Gabriel getting ready to announce the Day of Judgement. She retreated with wounded dignity and great squawking down the canal.

After stopping for breath on the bridge I looked down

towards the roadway leading to the nest. Liam was running towards me cradling two eggs, using his folded jumper as a basket. "Run, run, run," he shouted.

We ran for all our worth down the road. The distance to my house seemed interminable. It seemed as if we would never pass the hedgerow that secluded the tennis club on our left, although our strides were getting longer in case we were followed.

We passed Jimmy Davis from number forty-seven, a class-mate of ours, as we were running down the road. He was carrying shopping, obviously doing a message for his mother. He gave us a suspicious look over the top of his spectacles, but we ignored him and continued with our getaway.

We approached my house from the back lane. The gate was locked but I could see my younger sister through a crack in the door. I called to her and she unlocked the door, humming "Love Me Tender" to herself.

"Where were you for your tea? Mammy's looking for you. You've been up to something!" She was clued in on the adventure that happened with myself, Liam and the eggs.

She licked the Choc-Ice that was in her hand with big slurps. She nearly dropped it when we showed her our treasures. Her mouth and big brown eyes opened wide with disbelief when we showed her the largest bird eggs she had ever seen in her life.

"Don't tell anybody," I told her, "and if you do I'll tell that I saw you kissing Brian Byrne last Friday night behind the shed."

With a rusty nail we made holes at each end of the egg and blew the yolks free with our mouths. Liam and I, with the two swan eggs carefully ensconced in a cardboard box surrounded by cotton wool, were secretly delighted that our piracy was over and we had not been caught.

The evening clouds were gathering in over suburban gardens when Liam bid his farewell for home. In the kitchen in the house, my mother had left a salad ready for me since I was not present at tea-time. What with the excitement of the earlier escapade I was not at all hungry, and just sipped a cup of tea.

As I ascended the stairs to my bedroom an eerie feeling of remorse began to take hold of me. By the time I lay in bed waiting for sleep to arrive, it had become a full pang of deep sadness. My wrongdoing had come back to haunt me.

The sobs that followed made a soft damp stain on my pillow.

THE TROPHY

THE FOUR Winds Youth Club was a veritable sanctuary for me during this winter's soccer season especially on a Sunday night. It was the way for a righteous group of young blades on the north side of the city. From Cabra to Drumcondra, up to Whitehall across to Donnycarney and other adjacent districts.

The overseer of the club was a well-intentioned secular priest with a bald head and penetrating blue eyes that were full of life and good thoughts. He was Father Jim McManus who had passed through Clonliffe a number of years earlier.

His father was a butcher, well-off and successful. Father Jim's vocation in the world was looking after an old people's home in Dundrum and keeping a fatherly eye on his young brood of talented soccer players. This oasis was trouble-free – no parents, no maternal anxieties, no long list of rules to break a young man's heart.

In the left-hand rear corner of the major room which comprised the agreeable saloon, was a soft drinks and snack bar counter. A focal point of the venue was a coffee table, by the warm glow of coal, where a modest poker school was held. In the next room, equally pleasing to the eye, records and table-tennis were played.

Tonight at the eight o'clock was the final of the snooker competition. My opponent was Barney Donnelly. A lot of the girls in the local tennis hop fancied him, and I respected him as a useful outside-left and poker player. He was no pushover.

The trophy, mounted on an oak base, stood in a majestic posture on a table. It was silver-plated: the figure of a snooker player standing up clutching his beloved cue. A fabulous sight indeed. The figure had an expression of modest brilliance on his face.

A long established friend of the club, Mr Oakley, an English man with a podgy affluent face, smoked benignly on a cigar. He languished in an armchair beside the fire chatting to his wife and the padre, as he called Father Jim, which we all thought a bit odd.

The smooth green surface of the snooker table was alive with the clicking of balls, red and multi-coloured. It was the best of three games. There was a box of chocolates for the loser. Many pairs of eyes were rivetted on the drama. The tense atmosphere of the final frame, after the first two were split evenly, caused serious excitement in this small corner of the city.

The reds were potted in rapid succession on a fifty-fifty basis. But Barney's nerves were a little on edge. He turned on Whacker Nolan when he whispered into his left ear that a certain ball was available. "Who's playing this game Whacker, you or me? You'll get me disqualified."

But Barney was not that nervous. He got the yellow, the green and the brown. I got the blue and the pink which meant it was all to be decided on the black ball.

The shot being awkward, I played safe. Barney only half-connected with his cue on the white ball. In the momentary muted excitement that followed, the gallery and I thought that he was going to miss the ball altogether. He did succeed in making contact, but left the black ball hanging on the lip of the centre pocket. I aimed my shot as the words of an Elvis song came from the turn-table in the next room. "It's now or never..." The black ball clicked into the centre pocket. I had won.

At home the trophy was given a proud place on the mantlepiece in the living room. Aunts, uncles, brothers, sisters and friends admired it respectfully. The soccer season drew to a close. Spurs won the F.A. Cup, Everton won the League. The cold damp of winter had passed. Swallows were on the wing. The swans on the canal were sporting their family of six cygnets and the days became longer. Plans were being made for holidays and visits to the seaside.

A broken collar bone invalided me out of the summer vacation youth employment market. Contemplating lack of finances in the living room one bored summer's evening, I had an inspired idea. The trophy, I could hock it. There was no need to return it until September.

Three married women from the Corporation flats opposite Temple Street Hospital offered their husband's Sunday suits on this Monday morning, along with two candlesticks, bedspreads and three Foxford woollen blankets. The one nearest the counter and the tallest of the three, wearing glasses she got on the Blue Card, said "Ah Jaysus mister, make it three quid, ah go on. Sher, I'll be back on Friday once the husband comes home with the wages."

"That's if he doesn't spend the bleedin' lot in the pub," the smallest of the three said out of the side of her mouth so the pawnbroker, straining his cheek muscles in horror at the prospect of paying out three pounds, could not hear her. "Or worse, lose it on the horses!"

After some haggling and banter, the women left the room with the sour smell of poverty and headed in the direction of O'Meara's snug.

"Yes boss, what do you want to pledge? You're very young," he said in a rasping country accent. I carefully took the trophy out of my tartan-coloured duffel bag, which I used to carry my football gear, and placed it gently on the counter. In a voice feigning confidence, I enquired what price he might offer. The curt reply came back at the speed of light, "Thirty bob."

The style of the rapid transaction having been established by the clerk's clever and expert psychology, innocently I replied, "I'll take it."

As I walked down Dorset Street with the notes in my hip pocket this June morning, the world felt like a good place. The church of St. Francis Xavier, as I passed it, did not threaten my spirit with impending doom, as it usually did. Exam results were still a long way off yet, and I would fret about them when the time came.

The months of June and July were hot. The city sweltered with a heat wave. Sun-tans were awarded to most citizens, compliments of the Creator.

About mid-August, I met Barney on a long Drumcondra twilit evening in the park. He was with a young one I recognised from the tennis hop, Sheila Duffy. She was a little on the plump side with loads of freckles and flaming red hair. She was average height for a seventeen-year-old. I envied Barney. This son of Drumcondra had a double-edged message for me from Father Jim. Training was to commence the following week and I was requested to be present. The next part of the message was more dramatic. I was to bring the trophy with me. The new snooker competition was also starting.

That night, drawers and presses were opened and closed

and re-opened in a frantic search for the pawn ticket, but to no avail. It was definitely lost. This crisis, financial and physical, called for the intervention of a mother. The thirty bob was provided reluctantly from the maternal purse.

"You have no ticket," the pawnbroker said gruffly. "There is nothing I can do about it, you'll have to get a Court Order, that's the procedure laid down by the law," he said, a bit agitated.

"But you must remember the trophy I left in two months ago," I told him. "I have the money right here in my pocket."

"Sure those things are two a penny," he said pessimistically. "We get any amount of them through our hands."

Almost defeated, in the face of strong opposition, I parried with the plea, "Could you not just have a little look for it?"

He looked at me over the top of his spectacles. I could see there was a glimmer of hope in the situation, as he raised his eyes towards the ceiling. "You should have thought about all this before," he said. He sent his assistant upstairs to delve into the bric-a-brac of his wares.

The ten-minute wait that seemed more like an eternity ended with the assistant Sean, in his brown coat, waving the beloved spoils of the snooker art in the air. "Is this it?" he asked.

A lecture followed from Mr. O'Shaughnessy. "Now remember," he concluded, "you will not be able to redeem your property here again without a ticket."

In the final, the following year at the Four Winds, the entourage of supporters could not understand why I took my defeat by Mickey Ross so calmly. In my heart I knew my guardian angel had removed an obvious temptation from me.

MISHAP IN BANFF

THE TOWN was set 5,000 feet above sea level in the Rocky Mountains in Banff National Park. Around its perimeter the craggy peaks and ice-capped snouts reached into the sky.

The main thoroughfare of this tourist town was Banff Avenue – one main street that carried the load of traffic. A number of restaurants situated on the main drag caught like snapdragons the passing flight of tourists.

The town was a popular vacation employment venue for students seeking employment to pay their way for university. This they did in the nearby Banff Springs Hotel and local restaurants where the well-heeled tourists took in the sights in a setting of comfort and elegance

All manner of entertainment existed to attract the passing tourists and relieve them of their dollars. The Bow river snaked through the town at one end of the eastern side away from the Cascade Mountain, one of the highest peaks that overlooked the town below.

There was canoeing available on the river for a fee, nearby there was horse riding. Cable cars ferried visitors to elevated vantage points to savour the awesome spectacle of the mountains, a number of picnic tables in idyllic surroundings complete with wooden tables and seating facilities existed for the benefit of the tourists.

A tourist office dealt with any enquiries that might arise from the floating summer population. The town had a modern library that was only moderately used, a camera shop, a fire station, a school, a police station, a bookshop and a liquor store. It also possessed a number of bars. Chalets were dotted around the outskirts of the town and along river banks for the tourists' convenience.

In summertime a number of entertainers visited the town to entertain the tourists in the local hostelries. Attached to a local church there was a folk club-cum-coffee shop. No liquor was served. Poetry readings were also held there.

At one of the steak restaurants on Banff Avenue called Mr Steer I got a job as a bus boy cleaning tables. The owner was an affable sort of chap, German in origin. He made his money in the height of the tourist season, then headed to Palm Springs for the winter. Frau Weiner helped out in the restaurant when custom demanded it, as did her son who was a student at college.

I managed to get the job after spending my last few dollars on a meal, getting into conversation with a member of the staff, my own age and gender.

He clued me in that the owner was looking for people. After an informal interview with the boss I was told I could start work the following day. The next problem was a place to stay; I heard the chef next door in another restaurant had a space on a porch for rent. He agreed to give me the berth in his home in lieu of my first week's pay, the rent was reasonable and food was provided with the variable eight-hour shift at work.

A main feature of the eatery was a jukebox with the pop tunes of the moment being constantly repeated in rapid succession. Tom Jones's "My Delilah" was a favourite and played constantly by the young student clientèle in the early evening as they smoked McDonald's cigarettes and drank cokes and discussed their futures, the Russian invasion of Czechoslovakia, art, music, the Vietnam war and Pierre Trudeau.

The restaurant employed students of different ethnic origins and backgrounds: native Canadians from Hamilton, Toronto and Newfoundland, as well as those with Chinese lineage.

The female talent from the local School of Fine Arts was of a very high premium − artistically and physically. Through the summer I met many people passing through the doors of the restaurant on a casual fleeting basis − Australians, Americans, English, Scots, Irish and many others.

I used the library to pursue some of my literary endeavours. I had been trying to chisel a short story into shape for some time. It had originally been written in the winter chill of Reykjavik the previous year in my garret as I patiently waited for a job in one of that country's fish factories.

One by one I met the artists of the town and the mixed bag of the Bohemian community. There was Tom from Greenwich Village, a brilliant classical guitarist with an Irish father and German mother. There was Roger, whose aunt was loaded. He ran the bookshop as a joint venture with his friend Alex. There was George who was mostly just himself, a rather Rabelaisian personality with a thirst for life and a really passable socialist.

Gordon Lightfoot had just begun to be seriously launched on the folk world. Mike, a singer from Edmonton did great justice to his songs, especially "Railroad Trilogy." Of various females, one of the most alluring was Anna, an uncomplicated blonde sociology student from Montreal, whose honesty was as endearing as her sensitivity. One of my claims to fame was that I provided a tissue for her tears once when she was crying. But for the most part the heartbreak was concealed behind closed doors.

All through the summer people came and left the town. Business for traders was good. Summer romances amongst the vacation workers was a good crop of flowering *amour*. The tales of young love and friendship were developed and supported amongst the pine needles on the surrounding forest floor. Visits to the baths at the hot springs situated just outside the town were a popular activity.

Young people came from far and near to attend the highly esteemed Banff School of Fine Arts, idyllically situated on a mountainside overlooking the town itself. It had courses in drama, sculpture, painting, ballet and creative writing. I became friendly with one of the female students from the writing class. We both shared an interest in literature.

Roger from the bookshop was the resident poet in one of the saloons with an *avant garde* aspect to it. He acted as master of ceremonies on some evenings when Tom the classical guitarist and Mike the folk singer from Edmonton would entertain the variable-sized audiences. Visiting rock bands performed at the venue and consequently the audiences swelled.

The days were hot. The sun shone from clear blue skies with the occasional wisp of cloud. In the evenings the folk club called The Unsquares Cellar run by the local church group became a popular retreat and talented singers performed from the ranks of the students. They sang with their guitars. My first very painful attempts at reading poetry in public occurred among a number of other would-be poets from the School of Fine Arts. My knees trembled and I read with a high degree of self-consciousness in my voice. The response to this frightening ordeal was one of modest encouragement.

Roger was a considerable critic and a very tough one. He had passed comment in what I thought was a fair manner, on one of my short story attempts. He pointed out the lack of verbal display and the influence of Joyce, particularly the story called *The Dead*.

The night in question began unremarkably with one or two friends going to visit a small group of girls who lived in a chalet by the banks of the Bow river. Music played in the background and the conversation flowed. I was unused to a lot of alcohol, but that night I bought a bottle of Bacardi and began drinking it.

Slowly but surely my mind began swimming. For a while, although gradually becoming incoherent as my thoughts became confused, I thought I could cope. Then the alcohol began to rip my mind apart. I left the wooden chalet and stumbled through the woods into town. I felt a sense of impending disaster. I was fighting a losing battle for control with the alcohol.

I went into Mr Steer's where I worked. The place unsteady and weird with the music blaring from the jukebox. Now mentally I was at sea and the vessel of myself was floundering towards the rocks.

After about ten minutes sitting on my own I was joined by Roger the poet-cum-critic, Tom the guitarist and Mike the folk singer. The conversation that followed contained some pregnant and awkward pauses.

"Where were you tonight?" Tom enquired.

"I was drinking," I fumbled the word. "Where were you?"

Tom replied that the three of them had been doing a gig in the club down the street.

"Did it go well?" I asked. I again drawled my words. The

swimming began in my mind, but this time more rapidly.

"I read your poem," Roger began slowly. His piercing critical eyes peered at me intently. Somehow knowing what was to follow, I asked defensively.

"What did you think of it?"

The poem was called "The Future." I had written it in Toronto six weeks earlier. I thought it a good poem and I was proud of it.

"As a suture, it's not too bad," replied Roger.

"What is a suture?" I asked instantly.

"It's a surgical instrument for closing a wound," he retorted.

I had been depressed already, but this rebuttal was like a dagger in the back and then twisted mercilessly. I retired into myself in a deep melancholia and when I surfaced from the depth of my subterranean mood I was suicidal, dangerously so, as the large amount of alcohol had exacerbated my mood.

"Did you ever think of suicide?" I asked the assembled group nonchalantly, trying to conceal the inner crisis.

"It's up to you," Roger said.

I got up from my seat and walked down the street to the bridge with a 60 foot drop to the water of the Bow river. Something told me that it was not right to jump off the bridge into the water below, but something else was driving me, some powerful urge deep within myself. I turned on my heels and walked back down the street to the restaurant. I approached the trio situated at the table.

Tom remarked, "I thought you would be coming up for the third time by now." He laughed a kind of cruel condescending laugh and the others just grinned.

"Do you see any objections to suicide?" I asked, trapped

within my own black mood. No response was forthcoming. I again turned on my heels and went back to the bridge. Now there was no reprieve or interception from any source. Somebody passing by enquired about the correct time. I told him approximately and he passed on. I straddled the bridge wall sideways. It took all the courage I possessed to mobilise myself off the wall. I was on my way through the air, space and time into the unknown. The descent was longer than I thought. I was lucid mentally and knew that there was no reprieve, no safety net. I hit the water which was shallow, and some rocks. The alcohol was an anaesthetic. It saved me. I was alive.

With my right hand I pushed myself up to a standing position. My left arm and shoulder were in pain. I struggled out of the river which was shallow due to drought. I was aware of the blood pouring from my forehead. I walked back down the street into the restaurant and approached the trio who were still sitting down at the same table. They just gaped in disbelief and shock at the soaked figure in front of them, blood pouring from my forehead. The restaurant was practically empty. Somebody phoned for an ambulance.

In three days I was out of hospital. My only injury was a broken collar-bone. There was a certain discomfort while my injury healed, but strength eventually returned to my left clavicle and eventually things returned to normal.

The students returned to their various universities and with the first snowfall of the year I got a job in a hotel overlooking the valley. In due course I hit the road for Victoria, Vancouver Island: then California and more adventure.

THE EMIGRANT'S PRAYER

O Jesus,
Who in the first days of the life on earth
Was compelled to leave the land of thy birth
And with Mary thy loving mother and St Joseph
To endure in Egypt
The hardship and poverty of emigrants
Turn thine eyes in mercy upon our people
Who in search of employment
Are forced to leave their native land
Far away from all that is dear to them
And faced with the difficulties
Of a new life.
They are often exposed to grave temptation
And dangers to the salvation of their souls
Be thou O Lord their support in labour
And consolation in sorrow
Their strength in Temptation
Keep them loyal to their faith
Free from sin
And faithful to all their family ties.
Grant them that when life's journey ends
We may all be united
In the blessedness of our Heavenly home
Amen
Jesus Mary and Joseph protect our emigrants.

(Prayer read in churches in Ireland during the Fifties, especially
on Emigrant Sunday)

HE WALKED around the West End several nights in succession, his spirit wavering indecisively within him under the

strong influence of foreign experience and behaviour.

Hordes of people passed him on the streets but none of them could he call friend. He wanted to melt his being with one of the strangers who walked hurriedly by, and cause a union of friendship. He might as well have sought the crown jewels, so impossible was the desire.

There were signposts of direction contained in the night's experience. The first morning newspapers were on sale in Leicester Square, headlines of ill events happening in the country and the world.

Tom McEntee, from the north side of Dublin, was walking a narrow line of survival. He found its chances of success so fraught with a fragile accuracy that the only living creatures to whom he could communicate the depth of a very real anxiety which pounded in his heart were not human beings at all.

The creatures in question were the squeaks and squawks of geese, ducks and pelicans in St James's Park. They seemed to articulate like an orchestra the sounds of the city at night. Through the middle hours he felt in turn consolation, hope and despair. The dawn over the lake and the government buildings in Whitehall brought the presence of summer alive. It gave him a poetic insight into the God whose company he sought. In his soul that carried a leaden weight of perseverance he carried a blessing of hope.

The thing was so complex, accommodation problems, some sort of a job was not too difficult to get, yet he never seemed to get much leverage out of the money. Education, going to University in England was out of the question. He would not qualify for the grant as he had not the necessary length of residence in Britain.

Oh Sweet Jesus, why had he been born at all?

The experience of the young he met could provide libraries with books for decades, his own included. The strikingly handsome fair-headed young man he had met in the all-night café, Joe, aged twenty-three, from Sean McDermott Street, Dublin, had not lived in one permanent address in two years. "I could write a book about my experiences," he had said, combing each blond hair of his head neatly into place. The clubs, the women, the casinos. "I'm a male prostitute," he announced.

What kind of social system was this? Tom considered many times how the innocent suffered so severely. Money was vital to get out of his vulnerable plight. What had his old mate in British Rail said to him? "Tom, if you can't get a job in London, rob somebody, marry a rich widow. If you can't do it in London, then you can't do it anywhere."

At the time it had made sense to him. Now he knew he had to get out as soon as possible. He felt the situation was just a cleverly conceived, sophisticated trap. He was one of this jungle's most hunted animals, nobody knew the score better than him, just nobody. He was going to have to use his last drop of urban ingenuity to get out of this situation.

He walked past the plush hotels of Park Lane with the Mercedes and Rolls Royces parked outside. Down around Soho he was once or twice approached by the black or white prostitutes.

"Are you looking for a girl?"

He walked on around the neighbourhood. The moustachioed, macho, continental young men who solicited for the non-stop sex show inside. Topless bars, discos, expensive restaurants. He felt his loneliness within and how deep it went.

"Pussy-cat, pussy-cat where have you been? I've been to London and I find it obscene," he muttered to himself.

Around subway number four in Piccadilly tube station he had observed the community of junkies. "It's life and life only, it's alright ma, I'm only dying." He also made conversation with the community of winos outside the Empire ballroom in Leicester Square in the first light. They were friendly, with unshaven faces and hell written all over them. Then there was the community of homeless and vagrants at Charing Cross, sleeping out night after night in cardboard boxes and covered in newspapers.

At dawn outside the Department of Employment off Goodge Street, a queue of London's rejects and social outcasts would begin to form in search of casual employment on a daily basis. The money earned would buy hostel tickets in Bruce House at Holborn, St Mungo's or the Salvation Army in Peter's Street, in the shadow of Westminster Cathedral and the House Of Commons.

There were places that he could go to get help, but these places were controlled by rules and regulations. His experiences of such places as the Department of Social Security for people of no fixed abode made him understand they were part of the general sinister touch. He knew all the hostels for vagrants from the police cells at Bow Street and the two nights' accommodation in Centrepoint Refuge at St Anne's Church, Soho, to Dean St Reception Centre run by the Social Security. As he had no documented proof that he had been signing on from a labour exchange, he could not avail of the pittance he might receive. The reason for this was he had no fixed address – a vicious circle, a catch-22 situation, about which the man from the Social Security agreed.

He cast his mind back to a time when his parents were alive and he had a roof over his head. Even then there was not the privacy of his own room. His father's drinking had made it necessary for his mother to keep lodgers in the house. While in London he thought maybe he himself was an alcoholic, the stories he had heard at the AA meetings he went to, so many suffering people. There was also his partiality to soft drugs like marijuana and hashish to compound his difficulty. Now he was in his late twenties he had read an editorial in a newspaper about a young person's death, it went something like "human life does not always have a happy ending: being caught in the middle of a drama, the name of which was 'life' and God was the author."

He wondered about God's opinion on a lot of things. He must act and act fast and hope he would make the right decisions. There had to be a right answer, is that not what his schooling had been about, to arrive at right answers in real life situations? He had met Irish people in the Yukon, California, New York and Iceland. He was of a unique people with an authenticity, energy and strength for good, in spite of an island experience isolated in some dangerous way from more cosmopolitan places. He loved football – there was the time Alan Kelly played in goal, Ireland got beaten six-nil by England. It had been his dream that they should win. A better country, more natural resources. He cast his mind back to the Christian Brothers school he attended in Dublin. He knew the answer to the question, "what had been Ireland's economic difficulty?"

"Sir, Sir."

"Well, McEntee?"

"No natural resources, sir."

London was no safe protected soccer pitch or classroom with teacher or referee and concerned manager, where he played happily. This was the game of life, rough and dangerous.

He got up from his seat overlooking the lake in St James's Park. He would wait all day at Euston Station for the boat train to Holyhead.

He walked down the platform of Euston at 6.00pm. There was no ticket collector present. He fell asleep sprawled out on the seat of the train. On waking, the carriage was quite full of passengers. He began talking to a young Dubliner, John O'Donnell from the city centre area.

"Well, tomorrow I'll be in my own sweet Dublin," he said. "I walked all over London looking for a job, no luck."

Tom accepted a roll-up from John. They became friendly and Tom put John in the picture about not having a ticket. John had gotten his fare home from the Irish Centre in Camden Town. They rang his brother in Dublin and fixed it up. John waved the ticket at Tom, "I'm all set now."

Tom had thought about this ploy himself but he was in Sister Agatha Christie's bad books at the Centre. When his mother had been alive he had adopted this course of action. Now he would only get a lecture on work from the strict nun.

The train jerked towards Crewe and he was on his way, ticket or no ticket. He knew the main nerve centres of the journey very well from previous adventures – Rugby, Chester, Bangor, Holyhead. The ticket collector approached Tom, who explained his predicament. It turned out the ticket man was sympathetic.

"I will have to take your name and address and send you on the bill."

Tom breathed a great sigh of relief. The young Dubliner

opposite Tom was delighted with the outcome. Now for the old bill at Holyhead and the ticket man there. There were many different feelings of insecurity and Tom felt this was another. They were like specks of dust that shifted place with each other in the sunlit shaft of his soul. In spite of his insecure situation he felt hopeful and somewhat confident.

At Holyhead he waited until all passengers were on board. Thinking that there was no-one around he walked up the gang plank.

"Where you going mate?" asked the plain-clothes CID officer.

"Home. Dublin," replied Tom.

"You got a ticket then?"

No point in lying here thought Tom. "No, I don't actually."

"Then clear off," said the officer.

If at first you don't succeed, try, try again. Robert Bruce's story of the spider and the web came back to him.

All passengers were on board. Now things were quiet. He walked bravely up the gang plank again, nobody there, surprise, surprise, smiling broadly, the CID officer.

"Did you get a ticket then, Pat?"

Making apologies Tom retreated as fast as he could down the gang plank. He heard the policeman calling after him to "come back here and try that again and we won't be so kind to you."

It was worth one last try. The time of sailing was getting close. The mooring rope, that was it, he could climb the rope and make it aboard. He clutched the rope with his two hands and pulled himself forward as if he was on horseback. One slip and he would be in the water below and possibly knock his head against the vessel on the way down. He kept a low profile in the gents' loo until the ship was moving. He was on his way home.

He went up on deck and admired the full moon shining a silver path across the water. He reckoned the ship was equidistant between Britain and the Republic. He felt that as long as life was continued between both places there was still hope, in spite of accidents and terrible tragedy. He was still feeling very much alone, but still connected to the continent of humanity. How many times had he made this journey across the Irish Sea in his relatively short life? How many times had it been made by other Irish people? He felt he was a human being first, which made him a citizen of the world, yet the currents in his blood made him part of Ireland. His sister told him once that when his mother was living she would go down to Dun Laoghaire pier, take the sun, wait for the mail boat and hope her dear son would be on it returning home from England.

Back in his homeland now, he had to pick up the pieces of his crumpled life and allow his heart and soul to heal.

NUTS' CORNER

IT WAS NOT a club with formal membership and the ceremony of being nominated and seconded by a committee member, then signing an agreement to abide by all the rules, as with the gentlemen's clubs on St Stephen's Green. In the latter, club members are allowed to bring guests to dinner at their discretion, and, of course, contribute a sizeable financial consideration annually for the privilege, and each new member is sanctioned by a reputable person. By such process the riff-raff and undesirable elements are kept at a safe distance from the hallowed precincts of respectability.

But this confraternity of human liquorice all-sorts was a less formal gathering of illustrious souls, who, for reasons best known to themselves, had come together loosely under no particular ideology. Their meeting at the cross-roads of the world was a matter of accident to some extent. Some would say a case of the desperate meeting the misfortunate to share their common experiences.

This club did not keep minutes of the last meeting which the secretary read out at the commencement of the next meeting. There was no formal agenda for meetings with organised structure, points of order, going through the office of an appointed chairman, etc. One obvious absence in the structure of Nuts' Corner was a treasurer. This was a fitting anomaly as the members of Nuts' Corner invariably had no money, and they were usually dependent on donations from generous benefactors.

The location of Nuts' Corner has changed recently from its former site to the present one. This was due to a difference of opinion about philosophical belief with the management of a pub situated nearby. Two leading members took exception to the lack of credit facilities being afforded to the club's members. The outcome was a new venue for meetings of the society to conduct its business.

The main co-ordinators of the society, Cleary and O'Shane, were usually in session when other notables filtered into the proceedings. Cleary had a pint in front of him that had half-finished its voyage down the length of his glass, with a chaser of Jemmie and water. It was Tuesday morning and O'Shane with a Black Bush and a pint in front of him was the sponsor of the liquid refreshments. He had just collected from the "shareholders" meeting in Werburgh Street Labour Exchange.

They smoked at their leisure. O'Shane grinned happily to himself as he puffed a Hamlet cigar and Cleary rubbed his red whiskey nose while holding a Sweet Afton. It was half past eleven by the Roman numerals of the clock on the wall.

O'Shane spoke. "No sign of anybody yet," he said nonchalantly.

"It's early yet," replied Cleary, wearing his Crombie overcoat that was a little worse for wear, and a shirt and tie. "Don't worry," he added, "they'll be here alright. The troops will arrive," he said as knowingly as a fox contemplating the chickens below in a farmyard.

Then O'Shane, commenting on the residents of the Iveagh Hostel, the "hunting lodge" as he called it, said, "I think there must be a general release this time of the year."

He mused, "you never heard anything like it last night, the shouts and roars of them, they were like Apaches on the war-path."

The tall, venerable gentleman, a retired civil servant, Christopher, was the first to arrive through the door.

"Morning, Christopher," O'Shane and Cleary greeted him.

"Nice morning," replied Christopher, "but chilly and a bit frosty."

"Good morning for snaring rabbits out in the Wicklow mountains," said O'Shane.

"Or selling cattle at a fair in Listowel," said Cleary.

"Indeed, indeed," said Christopher sitting down and ordering a pint and opening his *London Times* crossword. The old man was highly strung, and delighted in gracious human sensibilities. His long life has taught him a preference for company that was familiar to him, although he was sometimes pleasantly surprised by strangers.

Bertie came down the bar from the entrance beside the bookie's office clutching the *Sporting Life* and sat down beside Christopher. Soon the pint, which the old man ordered, arrived.

"Judas has arrived," said Cleary to O'Shane under his breath. "The pox," he added.

The actor with his Roman head and barrelled torso came in and ordered a pint of Furstenburg. He had been in the early houses since seven o'clock, but was suddenly aware that he was running out of financial juice.

"Here's 'Peter O'Toole'," said O'Shane from the side of his mouth to Cleary. "Now what did I tell you, the troops will arrive."

Cleary and the thespian gentleman were not on good

terms, over a dispute between them the previous week, so a stony silence still ensued.

Shamie, the self-styled antique dealer and purveyor of arte-facts of a cultural nature, anything with which he might turn a shilling, carefully steptoed into the bar and took a stool at the counter at the other end away from the senior members of the society. All was not sweet with Shamie and Cleary. Shamie wore his usual peaked cap from under which, his eyes inspected and scrutinised the world. He ordered a cup of coffee and placed his satchel containing some prints of Dublin, for which he had a customer in mind, whom he was hoping to sell to later on in the day. The satchel also held a library book about the life of Chekhov for his own light reading.

The phone rang on the wall and Shamie, as he was in closest proximity to it, picked up the receiver and answered it.

"Hello, Cosmopolitan House," he spoke into the receiver.

"This is Una here. Is Brian Casey there?" said the young woman on the phone.

Eamon the barman looked down the bar at Shamie enquiring as to who the caller might be. Shamie lowered the receiver from his lip and said to Eamon the barman, "It's Una looking for Casey."

Eamon walked up the counter and said, loud enough for the earshot of Cleary and O'Shane, "the Duchess."

Cleary said under his breath to O'Shane, "The Duchess, I think she's resting at the moment in the asylum."

"Hello, Una. How are you? This is Eamon. How are you feeling?"

"I'm alright," said the young woman, "a bit better now anyway. The doctor says I'll be out in a week. Have you seen

Brian? Has he been in?"

"No sign of him today anyway," said Eamon.

"Tell him to ring me immediately you see him. He was supposed to come and visit me yesterday."

"Alright, I'll tell him. Bye, bye now, Una dear."

Eamon put the phone down and returned to washing glasses beside Cleary and O'Shane.

"The Duchess," said Eamon to Cleary and O'Shane.

"Is she within the walls?" asked Cleary of Eamon the barman.

"She'll be out in a week, with the help of God."

"She's in the right place alright," said Cleary accepting O'Shane's kind offer of another pint.

The newly arrived German artist to the city, Klaus, entered the bar. He had a much weather-beaten face, ravaged by booze and the elements. He spoke with a Germanic guttural accent. He was from just outside Munich and had come to Dublin via San Francisco. He ordered a pint of Furstenburg. Cleary in a low voice down the bar said to O'Shane, "Fucking Hitler is here now."

O'Shane replied smartly, "I think we have a quorum now alright."

Klaus began excitedly telling Eamon the barman and anybody else who might be interested. "I sold von of my paintings at the exhibition," he began. "It vas the furst painting suld. I got thurty Irish punts for it."

"Maybe now you'll fuck off back to vere you came from," said Cleary under his breath to O'Shane.

"Oh Jesus Christ," said O'Shane out loud in desperation, "Somebody should phone Maynooth and tell the Bishops. It's not fair in a Christian country, every day it gets harder in a Christian country, every day it gets worse in a Christian country. In a Christian country. In a Christian country!"

"My bollocks," he continued in a generous half-pretend, half-real rage, "My bollocks," he repeated, "it's Judas, not Jesus, who is running the country. And we are the real idiots," he confided to his lifelong friend, O'Shane. "You and me, we are the fools and idiots. It's enough," he said, grinning happily to himself and laughing inwardly, "to make you turn to drink.

"Absolutely right and correct, you're absolutely right," agreed O'Shane.

AN UNSAVOURY STORY

HIS BLACK HAIR was untidily brushed to one side, his looks were wolvish yet attractive to women, of whom he had more than his share. He sat in a corner of the public bar, drunk and becoming more so, as this was dole day.

It was his practice to get drunk every Tuesday, dole day. The manager-cum-owner had reminded him of the five pounds owing as well as the price of three pints of stout. Tuesday was the common day for the "shareholders" meeting to take place in nearby Werburgh Street and Thomas Street unemployment exchanges. As the day progressed the population of the pub increased. The patrons arriving who had no money and were on the dole, solicited drinks from those who had received their unemployment benefit that morning. These favours would be returned, possibly, if the moment was opportune and when the temporarily impecunious received payment.

The bookie Maguire arrived, sat at the counter and ordered a 7-Up. His mood was black after losses on the horses and his ulcer was acting up after a night of drink. He left his perch at the bar and asked the black-haired young man for some tablets to relieve his ulcer. These were provided; the bookie muttered his thanks and returned to his seat.

The black-haired young man swallowed some valium with his pint and gradually became incoherent. Two young men sitting at a table asked him if he had seen Reginald O'Toole recently as they had not seen him in some time. With a wave of his hand he told them that Reginald was doing a year in Mountjoy for fraud. At the counter Maguire had been studying form at Doncaster, the tablets having relieved his ulcer somewhat.

A group of senior alcoholics at a table in the public bar began discussing the merits of the food at the wine bar across the street where two of them had dined the previous evening.

A house painter of some repute, with heavy grey locks and a boozy face which he had spent most of his life acquiring, contemplated the remnants of his pint and wondered frantically where he would get another one. Still an hour to go before meeting his brother in The Sword on Camden Street.

The manager-cum-owner, smiling constantly, busily cut sandwiches and served drinks for the lunch-time office crowd in the lounge. He was in a good mood as business was good. A part of his brain privately calculated how much his investment would net this month.

Out on the street the weather was dry but cloudy. At brief intervals the sun penetrated through with the sporadic splashes of sunlight. A busker played his guitar with a repertoire of popular ballads from "When You Were Sweet Sixteen" and "Dublin In The Rare Ould Times" to "The Fields Of Athenry". He sang with great gusto from deep in his lungs and his voice carried the length of the street.

In the betting office on a corner adjacent to the pub, a moustached, curly-haired young man was marking up the board prices for Doncaster. An old woman fumbled with a bunch of yellow betting slips, trying the patience of the calm female clerk.

"I was wondering if there is anything on these?" she enquired.

After a brief pause the clerk replied with a knowing tone in her voice.

"No, Gracie, nothing. You had one winner in a double but the other one was only second."

The old woman, in a coat that had seen better days, rearranged her spectacles, took the useless dockets and said almost in a whisper of defeat, to a nattily-dressed city gent collecting a winning bet beside her at the counter, "Now wasn't that hard luck."

On the opposite corner of the street, diagonally situated, the news-vendor was busily trying to sell his wares. The evening papers had arrived with the news of a crime wave and a Southside residents' association requesting the government to take urgent action. Andy, the news-vendor, talked to two of his cronies about how jarred O'Kane, the car-park attendant on the street, had been the previous day.

"Yeah, I saw him," Andy said. "He was locked."

"I've seen him bad before, but I never saw him that bad," contributed Joey Madden, who at one time used to mark the board in the betting office.

O'Shaughnessy concluded the evidence for the prosecution by saying, "He was stocious. I don't know how he got home at all."

Andy added, "I'd say he's sleeping it off today alright."

The three laughed in unison imagining the mammoth hangover O'Kane was nursing somewhere.

Peter the barman tipped his cap to the news-vendor on the other side of the street whose trade was beginning to pick up. He stopped on his way up South William Street to have a few words with the news-vendor and Madden about the new proprietor of the restaurant further down the street.

Peter put a bright shiny millennium fifty pence coin into the outstretched palm of the unfortunate wino who was begging on the steps of the Powerscourt Town Centre. Peter recognised this man, who had steadily gone downhill from the time he began to lose his grip by asking for excessive amounts of credit in the pub.

"God bless you, sir," the wino said and attempted to create a smile displaying a row of bad teeth.

As he walked past the Powerscourt Town Centre, Peter was approached by another beggar of more distinction and gentility than the last. This one wore a passable suit with shirt and tie and highly polished shoes. He was a resident in one of the hostels on the North Circular Road run by St Brendan's Hospital under the care of the Eastern Health Board. He made daily excursions into the city centre to generate finance for drink and cigarettes. He acquired his money by begging. He had a slight deflection in his voice and enunciated his patter. "Excuse me, sir, could you spare ten pence? I am staying at the Iveagh Hostel." He was a former student of the leading Catholic boys' school close to the Green, and from a well-to-do family.

Peter was not taken with this punter's high airs and graces, so he passed with a rural shrug of his shoulders and left this one-time high denizen of the city to accost the next person on the footpath for alms. As he entered Clarendon Street Church he wondered seriously to himself why the world was so hard on beggars and the people who loved them.

Back in the public bar, the young man with the wolvish

handsome looks had fallen asleep. Reilly and Murphy, the two artists living on the dole, drank pints and discussed the forthcoming exhibition of their paintings that was shortly to take place on the premises. It was agreed that a well-known celebrity would open the exhibition. A gaunt poet listened attentively to their deliberations, partook of his pint, and at intervals asked questions and made suggestions about the publicity.

It was a foregone conclusion and the motion passed unanimously was that coming up to Christmas was the ideal time for the exhibition as there would be a plentiful supply of money to buy paintings. But frames and the printing of invitations would be a problem – as well as publicity, with so many events happening simultaneously.

When publicity was mentioned, the three young dynamos turned their gaze in the direction of the wolvish young man. It was well known that he had many contacts amongst the gentlemen of the fourth estate. But he was still out for the count.

The phone rang as the conversation was going on. Constable, the self-styled art dealer, dealing in artefacts of the antique variety, answered the phone.

"Hello, Intensive Care Unit," he said good-humouredly.

"Yeah, is that Swinford?"

"Yeah, this is me."

"Joey, is Derek Wooden there?" He was referring to the young man asleep in the corner.

"He is, yeah. But he's out for the count."

"Damn him anyway," began the voice of Swinford. "I'm up here in Castleknock. He was supposed to help me move two fireplaces to Francis Street. I had a buyer lined up and all. They are worth two hundred."

Constable was not really interested and said in a detached voice, "Try him tomorrow." On second thoughts he added, "I'll tell him when he wakes up that you called."

"Okay, thanks," said Swinford. "Be sure and tell him that I rang."

"Okey, dokey," said Constable, and returned to his pint.

Finlay, the Tailor, and Dignan, the Cavanman, returned from London, laughed heartily at the funny story for today. It concerned an Eskimo who got lost in a fog and ran his canoe up the arse of a polar bear.

Nobody in the bar recognised the two Special Branch men in the pub until they produced their identification and charged the owner-cum-manager under the Offences Against the State Act.

Sammy Gallagher told the plain-clothes men that he wanted to call his solicitor. They replied roughly that he'd have plenty of time for that down in the Bridewell. As Gallagher was frogmarched out the door into a waiting unmarked squad car, the genteel solicitor of alms passed Sammy on his way into the pub, his pockets rattling and bulging with change. He did not recognise the two plain-clothes policemen and said "Sammy, I'll pay you for those two pints I owe you for now."

"I'll see you later," replied a dejected Sammy as he left with his escort.

UNREQUITED LOVE

IT WAS approximately ten years since they first met in a city-centre coffee shop-cum-restaurant. She was then just out of school and working in one of her first jobs. He was recently returned from London after a long odyssey of poverty and hardship into the less socially acceptable levels of the Big Smoke's underground.

The city of Dublin was a complex maze of relationships, a network of intrigue, in business, social circles and cultural affairs. He was definitely in the less well-heeled sector of Dublin's bourgeois social grouping. Also most of his friends were students or recent graduates, starting out in their careers, mostly impecunious.

The coffee shop was on a street off Grafton Street, one of a chain of similar premises. It was popular with students and had a busy lunchtime clientèle of business men. The staff, for the most part, were students earning pocket money to help them through college.

She was not yet twenty-one, and rather new to the frontiers of city encounters and romantic interludes. How could she be otherwise? Shapely, with jet black hair, flashing intelligent eyes and a very quick mind, it was love at first sight. Her name was Alanna McIntyre from Glenageary, a reluctant and unwilling credit to the Loreto nuns. He was from Phibsboro, on the north side of the city, a wayward product of Christian Brothers education. They were from the same city but their backgrounds were very different. His was coloured by his late father's alcoholism and by mental retardation in the family, which led, not surprisingly, to a rebellious pattern of drug-taking in his own life.

He and Alanna made the most of their short time together. For him, he had never lived the fullness of the moment to its capacity before or since. There were visits to the cinema – Diana Ross in *Lady Sings the Blues*; *Diva*; the Theatre – *Long Day's Journey into Night* with Siobhan McKenna, Cyril Cusack; *The Merchant of Venice*. There were walks on spring afternoons through the National Botanic Gardens, through the foliage paths by the river, and visits to the hot-houses where she had begun studying horticulture.

There were glasses of wine sipped, appreciative of each other's company, in wine bars off Graftonia; pots of good coffee taken in the lounges of Buswells, the Shelbourne, the Berkeley Court and the Westbury. These helped relieve the less comfortable surroundings of the beau's one-room Corporation bedsit off Cork Street in the Liberties.

His heartbeat when the liaison was most intense was measured on the cardiograph of her friendship and affection. At some very special times in this Camelot of the imagination he could distinctly hear the chimes of wedding bells.

Seduction and all the pervasiveness of the permissive society did not permeate ultimately into their united world. Briefly she returned in the early stages of the romance, to his hovel. But the surroundings did not allow her to relax sufficiently to take off her coat. Later she announced what a terrible place she thought it to be.

Then the situation adopted a humorous aspect. The telephone was a medium of communication between them, was vital and essential, but it definitely only acted as a poor substitute for real meetings. Indeed the mechanical artifice only seemed to diffuse by articifiality, the sensitive nature of mutual feelings and love.

During the long trance induced by this nectar of love, life plodded on its weary way. People were born and their entry into the world celebrated in Church. Others died and were grieved and mourned with bitter tears and sadness. The young emigrated in greater numbers to Europe, London, Boston, New York. New romances began with great enthusiasm and were often terminated with accompanying heartbreak.

At different moments of meetings and partings they would exchange polite pecks of goodwill kisses which belied the deep and warm reservoir of feeling for each other.

Christmas, that emotionally charged time, was very special. Gifts were exchanged in a restrained display of affection and warmth. As he walked her to the bus on her way home she would say "I'll be alright now" and the angel of his dreams would fade into the winter night, with a parting kiss.

There was one social rendevous with some of her friends in a wine bistro in South William Street. The group chipped in for a bottle of cheap white plonk, he entertained them with funny stories as they gradually became tipsy.

Alone in conversation with her, tenets of religious belief were touched on. The point emerged that she considered logic to be the most important foundation in the complex web of living. He, for his part, the poet in him, tended to believe that feeling was the common ground of people.

All through the changing emotional climate of their friendship, he wrote poems for her. This he did usually late at night in his den in the Liberties. Letters were exchanged reporting altering fortunes of friends and family as well as the state of personal well-being.

About midway through the life-span of their *amour* he was accepted as a mature student for a Liberal Arts Degree at St Patrick's College, Maynooth. She wrote him a letter of encouragement to pursue and complete the course of studies. He got a flat in Maynooth, but lack of money, and his own emotional turmoil, made the task of studying impossible.

It was a bright oasis in an otherwise unsuccessful academic career. He had a part in a Jean Anhouil play, *The Lark*, staged by the Maynooth Drama Soc, which heightened many dull lives on the campus. She attended the performance and enjoyed the production immensely. Occasionally he had a literary success − in print or on the airwaves. These short-lived achievements seemed to consolidate the friendship and outweighed his lack of steady, permanent, pensionable employment. Their mutual personal lives as they affected each other had remained constant and positive and augured well for the future. Loyalty between them had been tested once or twice to breaking point but there had been no break.

Just, perhaps, a fracture of emotion when she began doing a steady line complete with the "etceteras" of any serious relationship. He was a romantic and an idealist and was happy deep within himself to receive even the residue of a great love in the hidden corners of his imagination. He gently rekindled love's flame by lighting a candle for her in a church, or perhaps quietly pining for the pleasure of her company in solitary reverie late at night.

But now reality was turning on its axis to dislocate his

dreams and longing for her. A dream, delicate and human like a cloud of hope, sailed across his heart and soul. Maybe if he really tried he could sever the memories of her, but that would also kill the very breath of life within. It enabled him, like a vehicle of purity and truth, to travel unharmed through all the murky and polluted waters of corruption — the tainted pools of which he could perceive drowning people all around him.

Within the pages of their story together, through incomplete sentences of communication, utterances of separate lives, he wished to break through the boundaries of the heart's imprisonment. He hoped to overcome, with an outburst of truth, his human cage of isolation. Otherwise he would be reduced to the mediocrity of a life that had never really and truly known love.

She still stood for him as an illuming light that spread like a fan and lit a dream that had come to fruition. His love was a ripe fruit tree in an orchard from which the fruit would never be plucked. It had been planted and grown, tall and strong, and now he hoped it would outlive less authentic flowers of the soul and survive with a strong scent of respect and sincerity in his heart.

ST ANTHONY AND
THE FALSE TEETH

BEN LEIGH DRIVE lies in a complex network of similarly named streets in Scarborough, Toronto, an area affectionately known to Torontonians as Scarberia, because of its outlying location. My brother Desmond and his lady Daphne live about midway down this street, with their dogs, Tramp and Hobo; a yellow canary called Marmalade which has the happy habit of singing delightfully in the morning; and a cat whose name is Gilbin, who is wont to roam freely.

It's the venue at Christmas for a major gathering of three or four families and extended families, nieces, nephews, uncles, aunts, grandmas, cousins, etc. etc. I have known happy times in this house, as have the many guests who have passed through its doors.

The room allocated to me was set at the rear of the house, small but comfortable, and adequate for my needs. For most of my visit, calm and normality presided over events until the dark hour when I woke one morning and I was unable to find my false teeth, what with a few seasonal drinks the night before.

It was not the first occasion that the molars went missing. As much as I allowed myself to think about it, there would be a repeat prescription of justice in finding them. The initial two searches of the room proved fruitless. After two or three more searches the situation was a matter for concern.

My brother Desmond's nerves were frayed at all the edges.

His colleague and good friend with whom he had been working for many years, Kyle, had not been in touch for days. He feared the worst as Kyle lived alone and he was going to call in on him. Kyle always phoned. Des was high on the Richter scale of panic.

Des dictated, "Drag everything from the room piece by piece, then go over it with the vacuum cleaner. Those damn teeth have to be there. While you're doing that I'll go over in the truck and call in on Kyle."

Thoughts of Kyle's welfare also darkly occupied my mind, double trouble, the worst kind. Suddenly all the storm clouds were brewing at the same time. Disaster was imminent and there would be havoc unleashed.

How could I be so incompetent as to lose the molars? I dragged every item of clothing and personal property from one room to the other, piece by piece. Then I stripped the bed, looked under it, turned it upside down, looked under the mattress – this was much worse than being a monkey in a cage on a wet Sunday afternoon in the zoo. Anyway, monkeys don't lose their dentures.

I entered into a slow decline, down a dark ravine of depression, as I disbelievingly returned all the clothing and personal possessions from one room to the other yet again.

Des's truck pulled into the driveway. The yard door slammed hard with what seemed like a mixture of depression, frustration and a little anger.

Des had returned from his mission. The worst had happened – Kyle was dead. Des was very upset. As he spoke his words were heavy with emotion. "The janitor let me in. His face was blue, the poor guy, he must have been there for a few days. My old buddy, I'll miss him," he said, as he fought back the tears.

If I wanted to cut short my visit there would be a two-hundred dollar charge by the airline to bring the flight forward. This was beyond my meagre resources. The local denturist had priced me out of the market with my limited resources for a new pair of dentures.

Des and I sat in the kitchen of the little house that had known happy times. We sat on the high kitchen stools facing each other, clutching a large vodka apiece. After the morning that was in it, we richly deserved them, both of us.

Des gulped a little for air as he spoke, trying to relax and reconnect with normal emotions after the high-pitched tension of the morning's ordeal. "It's a shame all the same, you going to Boston and all, those high society ladies and the pretty girls in New York — no teeth."

"It could be worse," I replied glumly.

Having thought about it previously for some time and when Des was out of the kitchen for a few minutes, I put my plan into action. I said three Hail Marys to St Anthony in one last desperate bid to redeem the apparently hopeless situation.

Des returned to his perch on the stool and poured another drink. Whether it was my hand reaching around my back to scratch it in some lazy useless movement; or I was being directed by a higher power, I felt something stuck half-way up my woollen jumper. As I touched it, I felt like a drowning man would feel as he grabbed onto a twig in a fast-flowing river. It felt like a denture. I retrieved it slowly and held it up in the air for both of us to see, to inspect and enjoy.

Again, I put my hand around my back and there was a second denture. Des and I laughed with joy, relief and pleasure. What could we do except laugh after the previous hell we had gone through together during the dramatic events of the morning?

AMERICA, HOW ARE YOU TODAY?

AFTER ARRIVING at JFK, with a copious supply of my short stories, I find to my delight that there is a welcome for Irish literature in the Irish bars in Manhattan, like Eamon Doran's on 53rd Street and 2nd Avenue.

Manhattan at Christmas: the lights of the trees on the streets tingle and sparkle like the shining crystal of entrepreneurial eyes studying their prey. Beautiful, like the eyes of a wolf in the darkness preparing for an attack.

Welcome to the isle of Manhattan where concrete towers of skyscrapers protrude into the evening skyline – a memorial to the white man's commercial assault on the dignity of the American Indian, who exchanged the entire panorama for a handful of beads.

On the following day I met a friend, Paul Tilak from Dublin, a comic by profession, in the Chelsea Hotel. It still has an artistic thrust to its clientèle, with a commercial tariff for mummifying dead celebrities.

At Port Authority Greyhound bus depot in Manhattan as the Christmas queue elongates like a caterpillar's tail, the announcements of the departing buses to North Carolina and Jackson, Mississippi, are underway. A mass of black folk are returning to the South after a long year earning a living in New York city. Similarly from Boston in New York, Irish emigrants are returning to villages and towns all over Ireland. But, I would opine, probably more prosperous.

Homelessness is alive on the streets of New York, Toronto and Boston. In the American cities a high proportion of young and middle-aged, black and white, are homeless. This year's less severe winter means that they will have a little respite from the rigours of hypothermia and related problems.

A retired radiologist gentleman from Acapulco, Mexico, whom I meet on the fifteen-hour bus journey from Toronto explains excitedly how he is amazed that people can live in such cold. "I've never seen snow, I just came to see it. People must be crazy to live in this weather. Come to Mexico. You have the sun, cheap beer and pretty señoritas."

In Boston I learn that a lot of graduates from institutions of higher learning in Ireland can wield a paint brush, operate a vacuum cleaner, or pull a plug. Some with advanced degrees have found a perch as research librarians in a grove of Academia like Boston University.

On Broad Street in Boston, in a pub like Mr Dooley's, visiting poets from Ireland are given a cordial welcome and response. The audience includes Patrick Walshe, formerly assistant ambassador at the American Embassy in Dublin; Brendan Frawley and his wife Maureen, two good friends of many young first-time pioneers from Eire. Pat Grace in the L&B, the little bar in Boston (47 Provence St) has offered the hand of friendship to many far from home. Boston is home of the famed Omni Parker House Hotel, within a stone's throw of the site of the Boston Massacre. The old state house of the British overseers is adjacent.

Among those who changed the course of history who have worked at the Parker House Hotel are Malcolm X and Ho Chi Minh, who also worked in Jamet's Restaurant, Dublin, in the early 1920s. In the Last Hurrah bar downstairs, Joe Murphy the bartender quips, "John Hume sat in exactly the same seat you're sitting in last week." President Mary Robinson was also a visitor. In the words of Oliver Wendall Holmes, "such guests, what famous names its record boasts." Its literary club included Longfellow, Thoreau and Ralph Waldo Emerson. The *Atlantic Monthly* magazine, founded in 1857, was the result. Sarah Bernhardt was a guest, and Alexander Graham Bell would stay nowhere else. Chief among its personalities has to be JFK. He took his first step into public life and politics by announcing his candidacy for Congress in its Press Room. But the mob of ghosts which include Charles Dickens does wander.

Compared to the Sixties and Seventies, America has a new cautiousness and conservatism now. The concern over jobs is uppermost, meeting the mortgage payment or getting the children through college and into good earning positions. Republican victory in Congress shows a creeping movement towards the right. From within the ranks of the Democratic party, there is growing opposition to President Clinton's $40 million rescue plan for the Mexican peso.

On Martin Luther King remembrance day, a national holiday, most of the commercial life of the nation ingloriously remains unabated. "I have a dream, the lamb shall lie down with the lion." But the American Eagle is still ready to pounce in the name of free enterprise.

The way in which Irish culture and music has assimilated with Afro-American forms can be savoured in places like Paddy Reilly's pub on 28th St and 2nd Ave. Eileen Ivers is on the fiddle, a black drummer accompanying her. This is also home from time to time of Black 47, Pierce Turner and Steve Duggan. They join musically with a great variety of ethnic groups from New York. Over a pint at 4.00am, it's a joy.

The last chores include a radio talk show on the popular Adrian Flannelly Irish radio programme, transmitted to 1.2 million people in New York. A visit to the East village, contacting some publishers on Madison Ave. A visit and a private prayer at the spot where John Lennon was shot. America – Imagine!

Going through the toll bridge on the New Jersey turnpike, I'm heading into white middle-America and its suburban environs. Nearby is Newark airport; the lights of metal fire-fly planes queue up to land in single file from the western horizon. They are rather like flying creamery carts in an Irish dawn, hovering outside a rural co-op.

How are you today? Have a nice day.

Little Silver, New Jersey
19 January, 4.00am, 1995.

IMMIGRATION

HE HAD HITCHED down to Biloxi, Mississippi and waited outside the town as he headed to New Orleans. The lift he got proved to be his last in the USA. It was the first woman driver he had met on his odyssey from the East Coast. After the preliminary niceties from the hitch-hiker's book of etiquette, he realised they were being followed by a police car with sirens blazing.

The cop made the woman pull over to the kerb, proceeded to tell her she was speeding and he got busted for vagrancy. The court was in the rear of a fishing tackle store. After an enquiry by the magistrate as to whether or not he had five dollars, he was taken to the local county jail and locked up.

The following day Immigration paid him a visit at his new residence and temporary address. He told the Immigration officials how he jumped ship, which was quite common. He was then taken downtown by New Orleans Immigration and placed as an inmate of the notorious New Orleans Parish Prison. The two Immigration officers warned him: "Be cool, there are some tough cookies in there."

The jail, that was to be his home for the next seventeen days, proved to be quite an education. It was a segregated prison, conditions were poor and the building was very run down. The cages ran round a cat-walk on the ground floor, with a separate communal area on each side for meals, recreation and exercise.

Jail was a lonely place that filled him with remorse and guilt. The inmates were really a great cross-section of the American underworld with all types and varieties of criminals – from the Japanese heroin dealer to George, who was in for psychiatric observation and who played chess across the corridor at night, to Louis, who was in for armed robbery.

A special cell existed for the gay population, who nightly conducted debates and discussions, with the theme that women more or less ruled the world. The food was poor. The diet mainly consisted of beans, rice, salami, coffee and boloney. Louis taught him to play chess. When he mastered the rules they played a game He checked Louis in the first game. Louis remarked: "Kid, you learn fast." But Louis won the game.

There were books to read at night while the prison slept, like *Man against Himself* by Karl Menniger, some of the writings of Ralph Waldo Emerson, the story of El Cordobes, *I'll Dress You in Mourning* and *The Shoes of the Fisherman* by Morris West.

He was interviewed by a senior Immigration official and offered voluntary deportation home. He was told that he could go to any country in the world, except the adjacent countries like Canada or Mexico. He rather fancied Brazil but that would take a long time to come through.

During the day he occasionally joined in the poker game, but without much success as the card school was made up of seasoned professionals. Sometimes fights broke out between the prisoners, brief and sporadic but very vicious. He met a German youth who had been a steward on a tanker. He was facing a year on some petty charge. Then there was a Jehovah's Witness who had refused to go to Vietnam because he did not believe in war.

The cheap black-and-white convict's clothes seemed to

soil and spiritually interfere with his sense of self-respect and pride as a human being. He was debased as a human creature to the level of a trapped and frightened variety of rodent. It was a microcosm of the world, the pettiness, jealousy, greed, envy and avarice. But there was friendship, loyalty and even love among his fellow prisoners.

The justice was rough, tough and primitive. The huge iron electric doors slammed shut firmly at night. He felt that it was the door of the human heart that was being closed on him. He was different from the other prisoners by accident of birth and origin. The ridicule and mockery of his accent, while it hurt him painfully, made him tolerant so that he regularly defended the black inmates in the other cell block across the yard in the segregated wing.

Seventeen days later he was told to collect his property. As he walked out through the big iron doors of the cell block some of the friends he had made cheered loudly enough to lift his heart. He was going to be free. Freedom was the greatest drumbeat of the soul.

Outside the jail while walking towards the waiting car he let out a string of expletives. The small fat Immigration official heard him and retorted: "Now, Tom, if you'd done nothing wrong, you wouldn't be in there."

At the airport he was introduced to a PR man from Eastern Airlines, in the care of whom he would get a plane to New York.

"You from Ireland?" the man said. "Yeah, we get all the celebrities through here. Last week we had Batman from Gotham City."

The final word from the officials were, "Now, Tom, when you get to New York you'll be met by two Police officers. Stay on the plane until everybody has disembarked. Got that?"

So he found himself in the air, flying over the winding Mississippi river on the first stage of his journey home. When the plane landed at JFK, two Feds entered. "That's our man."

He was then taken downtown to the local lock-up until the time arrived for the Aer Lingus flight to Dublin. The two cops were told by the sergeant on duty, "Now, you tell them at Aer Lingus that you want some Irish coffee."

The plane took off from the airport and arrived at 5.00am at Shannon. Later came the flight to Dublin. The colours of the dawn were spectacular, with the morning sun rising over the Atlantic and the green fields and hills of Ireland. Through the window he saw Dublin Bay shimmering like a glittering bowl of crystal below him and the city of Dublin with its rooftops and beaches.

He waited in line for his luggage. The cardboard box arrived with the legend "FEDERAL PRISONS OF AMERICA" emblazoned on it. He diplomatically went to the head of the queue and picked it up to avoid embarrassment. He went to the Gents' loo and changed his shirt. No money for a taxi.

He knocked on the door of the terraced house. His sister answered it.

"Tom," she exclaimed excitedly.

"I have a taxi waiting. I need ten bob."

She got her purse, as she was working for an insurance company now, and he paid off the taxi.

He went into the room where his mother slept. It was still quite early in the morning. He could see she was delighted to see him. His father was there with a bottle of whiskey in his hand. He was completely drunk.

AN EVENING WITH
LOUIS ARMSTRONG

"JAZZ," to quote Fats Waller, "is like an orgasm. Unless you've had one, you will never know what it is." Life, as we all know, whoever we are, no matter what we do, is full of jazz, the up-beat and the down-beat, virtuosos and sometimes a stunning solo.

I was approximately twenty-one years of age in June in Toronto, 1968. I had spent the previous winter and spring in the environs of Reykjavik, Iceland. The work had been tough , both on the small Icelandic cod-boat out of Grindavik, south of Reykjavik, and as a fish-factory hand.

The employment gave me the money to fly to New York and hitch-hike via Detroit to visit my long-lost brothers in Ontario's major city, Toronto. My eldest brother, Leo, was my first host on the early part of my excursion into the fast-growing city of Toronto, that has since become the fifth biggest metropolis in North America.

All the barriers of age and generation were securely and firmly brick by brick walled up between myself and my older brother. So much so that there did not seem any hope of a reprieve, no happy communication and the vestiges of brotherly love. The relationship was taking a nose-dive towards a point of no return. We needed a thaw in the ice and some clemency for our mutually, deep, entrenched points of view. They were also coloured by family dissent in the mother house at home in Ireland. Enter Louis Armstrong and the All–Stars.

They were playing the Ambassador Club on a hot summer night in downtown Toronto. The musicians flexed their musical notes, with the Filipino drummer in good form, tapping his skins adeptly and skillfully, beating out the rhythms of his heart and soul.

A short time into the musical fray, Louis Satchmo Armstrong appeared stage centre, a Mandarin of geniality and a physician of human ills and a healer of the unclean spirits of despondency, with his cherubic smile and flashing white teeth.

New Orleans, Basin Street and Bourbon Street was the cradle, as far as I knew, of Satchmo's early jazz experience and of black culture of the Deep South. A little over a year previous to this evening in Toronto, I had tasted some of the bittersweet injustice of a New Orleans jail, with its strict code of segregation. I had heard a black woman from a nearby cell calling out for her baby in the middle of the night. What she had been trying to articulate, I surmised, was now finding a voice in the music I was listening to.

The ice between my brother and myself was melting like the snow of an Icelandic winter in springtime. I confided in a moment of lucidity to my brother, "This music is born out of the experience of the poor." He just smiled benevolently, continuing to enjoy himself hugely, as the tempo increased on stage and Satchmo blew out his magical notes of blues and jazz. The feeling struck deep home that this was no ordinary experience I was privileged to hear. This was a very important night in my life.

The large white handkerchief appeared as the trumpet lay

at its ease on one side of his bulky torso. The coal-black face of this mine of talent was lathered in sweat, after the very hard work of once again giving and giving to people – no matter who they were – black or white, happy or unhappy, Jew or gentile.

The musicians had left the stage. I discreetly and tactfully retired stage right to try to negotiate an autograph. I was in luck. The tall formidable black figure of the security guard bade me welcome at the star's dressing-room door. Satchmo, seated behind a table, courteous and friendly, asked to whom did I want the signature signed. For my nephew Stephen. "Is that Stephen with a PH or a V?" "PH," I replied.

For this brief interlude I was alone with the black Pope of art and jazz. I offered my thanks and as a gesture of good-will, I asked, "When are you coming to visit Dublin, Mr Armstrong?"

The bass voice replied happily and warmly, "Boy, I played Dublin in February".

I will always remember that night and how barriers and broken bridges can be mended and healed by the right kind of giving.

TORONTO 25 YEARS LATER

"IT WILL BE a great town when it's finished," quipped Brendan Behan, the playwright, about Toronto. As yet unfinished, this major Canadian city has become an important international metropolis.

On my last visit, I had achieved landed-immigrant status without undue difficulty. I was then newly-arrived in Canada from Iceland via New York. That was in May, 1968.

I went to work as a steward in a golf club in a Toronto suburb which then had full employment. My varied duties included serving drinks, cleaning, dish-washing and keeping the spiked golf shoes spick and span. The minimum wage then was $1.25; now it's $6.80.

Time changes cities, countries, and the visitors who for different but similar reasons seek admission at their frontiers. There is a multi-cultural society here which should be, and is, a source of some pride.

During the late Sixties, the era of my first visit, Toronto's Yorkville was a hippy cultural centre which nourished and developed the careers of Leonard Cohen, Neil Young and Gordon Lightfoot. The Sixties aura has been eclipsed by Yuppiedom to become a well-heeled centre of fashionable commerce, like the Portobello Road in London, Fifth Avenue in New York or Grafton Street in Dublin.

At the time of writing, the temperature is -16°C and the wind chill factor makes the cold feel Siberian. But through the preceding month, there have been pet days too, rather like a clement Irish spring day. Ma Claus, an irreverant invention by the local business community, had left with her spouse, Santa, on a sleigh for their home in the Arctic. Christmas decorations have been replaced by January-February sale signs and unbeatable bargains. Torontonians may be a conservative breed in many areas, but not when commerce and business are to the fore. Then the knife of a sophisticated business surgical acumen is activated.

This city and its two million inhabitants (four million in the Greater Toronto area) have not escaped the recession unscathed. Unemployment, homelessness and crime have reached new levels. True, criminal activity is nowhere near American urban proportions – as in Detroit, Washington, Los Angeles or New York – but hold-ups and break-ins are now more sinister and brazen than Torontonians have ever known.

In Ireland, success in the World Cup is uppermost in the national psyche, while in Toronto the Blue Jays baseball team's win in the World Series is comparable to Irish pride in Jack's Army. This is also the season of ice hockey, with every youngster on lake and pond wielding a hockey stick and cherishing secret ambitions of being a million-dollar-a-year National League pro, playing with the Toronto Maple Leafs.

Via satellite from Dublin, CBC-FM's Writers And Company programme features Dermot Bolger, historian Roy Foster, Edna O'Brien and John McGahern. Roddy Doyle is a hot literary property (number 2 on national best-seller lists with *Paddy Clarke Ha Ha Ha*). Film director, Jim Sheridan's *In the Name of the Father* is unanimously acclaimed and Daniel Day Lewis's 19-year-old face beams from posters in every subway station.

Jimmy McVeigh's Irish pub, The Windsor – mother house of music, news and gossip at Church and Richmond – is an acceptable local venue for fun and meeting. Customers are a diverse bunch from widely different backgrounds with multi-coloured hues of interest. In previous times, to attain landed-immigrant status – a highly-prized trophy – was never too difficult, though never simple: concealed and unsuspected hidden skeletons can surface and chase away all hopes of legality.

Missing home, family and friends as well as coping with feelings of loneliness are normal occupational hazards for every immigrant. Many would rather be at home but economic realities overrule the heart. There are real problems to deal with: accommodation is expensive; the first or second job is often far from ideal; and adapting to a totally new environment can render life awesome to the new initiate from Ireland. The prospect of launching into the unknown with all its hidden pitfalls can shake the strongest person.

A relative who has an electrical sign business and works outside in sub-zero temperatures soon creates for me the reality of the worst winter in years. The cold closes down Pearson International Airport for the first time in recorded history. The sign business is lucrative, with a great variety and amount at every street plaza and corner. Not so tempting is climbing a forty-foot ladder with the wind chill down to – 20°C. These are professionals who install eight-foot fluorescent lamps at this height, with the dexterity of a pro ice hockey player knocking a puck around a rink.

There is a quintessential difference about being broke in a city like Toronto as opposed to Dublin. One example: if you find yourself without a subway token, for whatever reason, at the time of the last train, the feeling is that you are about to sink into the bowels of the earth and never return. This is particularly true if you've taken a few drinks.

In Dublin, there would be a safety net due to familiarity of place and people.

Not having a dollar strikes in the heart as not being able to ascend the golden stairs to heaven and economic salvation. And there is no reprieve or absolution from material dispossession.

The purpose of my visit here is to test waters present and future for related literary work, readings and so forth at colleges and universities.

During my stay, there is a spot with a high profile programme on CBC Radio with Catherine O'Hara. A phone call leads to a fifteen-minute live interview of talk and poems on CIUT-FM, the University of Toronto station. There are poetry readings for which I have been engaged at York University, the Irish Canadian Cultural Centre, the Idler Pub, the El Mocambo (a rock venue) and the U of T.

I accept an invitation to read privately for an Irish couple, Paddy from Belfast, and Deirdre from Downpatrick and their circle of friends. It helps generate income in a world of diminishing returns.

Irish culture is represented in one particular grove of academia very competently by Professor Ann Dooley, chair of Celtic studies at St Michael's College, University of Toronto. Professor Dooley offers courses of a Celtic and historic thrust which serves the emerald isle admirably. In common with other universities, it is seriously underfunded.

The Irish Canadian Cultural Centre on Dupon Street has a lively and talented dramatic entourage with forthcoming plays by Graham Reid and a new Dermot Bolger script. A visiting neurosurgeon from Cavan via North Dakota is in the company along with a psychiatrist from Armagh.

Pubs with names like The Artful Dodger, The Duke of Kent, The Rose & Crown and The Duke of York are homes for ex-patriates from England, Wales, Scotland and Ireland. The emphasis on food in bars as well as drink is a very evident slice of business practice.

While Alexander Fleming, it is widely known, discovered penicillin, it is also true that insulin was discovered in Toronto by Nobel Prize winners Best and Banting in 1922 at Toronto General Hospital. The city's modern downtown hospitals include the renowned Hospital for Sick Children, the envy of other world-class cities.

The Ireland Fund with offices on Front Street provides financial support for projects in both the north and south of Ireland. Under executive director Paul Farrelly, the theme is Peace, Culture and Charity. The organisation brought Roddy Doyle to Toronto and the Irish Canadian Cultural Centre was packed on two consecutive evenings.

If Toronto was a city unfolding at the time of Brendan Behan's visit in the Sixties, it is now a liner of great proportions and style that has arrived safely in international waters. It can weather any storms coming its way.

Just like Sodom and Gomorrah and the Roman Empire, all major cities have a hidden agenda of personal and general destruction, and Toronto is no exception.

THE PATIENT'S VIEW

AT THE HEIGHT of his fame, Brendan Behan remarked, "The world is divided into two categories of people – there are nurses and patients. I'm a nurse." The statement invites the question, What are the qualities of a good nurse and, indeed, what is the criterion of a good patient?

Commendable virtues that might be considered are courage and a sense of humour. They are indeed complementary to each other. In Ireland we are fortunate because we possess them in abundance.

Having worked in hospitals and also having been a patient, I know they can be the best of places and also a place sometimes from which you feel like you'd like to make a fast exit. Nowadays a very important priority in a hospital is the charter governing patients' rights, a guide that cherishes the individual dignity and rights of the patient.

Things can sometimes go terribly wrong, both for patients and doctors, with serious consequences. The daily papers frequently record some very unhappy cases, but what is not highlighted is the relief and comfort that doctors and nurses provide in their daily round of chores. One is left with the strong impression of the extraordinary variety of help available to people, myself included.

A feature of the modern casualty department is the number of security personnel. Patients do not volunteer to be handcuffed or placed in custodial care. The uniformed security staff use mobile phones to relay messages to their colleagues. "That's a rouge" may mean, "I'm on my own here, I need help! Half the city has showed up under the influence of drink and drugs."

Mr Drink and his girlfriend, Miss Drugs, will be doing a steady line into the new millennium. Perhaps until the time, while under the influence of stimulants, they crash into each other, coming from opposite directions on the Naas dual carriageway, and so disappear in a bonfire of smoke and flames.

But in this little place we call the world, there are bogey-men and so, alas, also bogey-women.

The definition of a bogey-man might be the guy who is going to solve the world's problems after he sinks the next pint. The kind of guy who will tell you exactly what you are doing wrong - in a way that makes complete sense to him and nobody else. A sailor on a sinking ship, God bless him and all who sail with him!

Recently through my letter box was delivered my medical card: a simple rectangular piece of plastic with my name and number printed on it. This innocuous piece of plastic is a great relief to receive for somebody not necessarily a senior, but shall we say past his junior years. The impending physical ills of the future will be given every chance of defeat with the right treatment applied – and who amongst us does not share a similar ambition to live as long as possible?

In America, the land of the free and not so free, many are plagued by exorbitant medical bills. In the adjacent land of Canada the same often unaffordable expense obtains. This innocuous piece of plastic with a number and a name, provides access to medical treatment until such time that something I write or a win on the lotto gives me access to a million.

The recent strike action by nurses was deserving of the widespread public support which it received, and the agreed settlement is welcome. Now the cat is among the pigeons – or maybe the sharks and the vultures – for similar claims by the teachers and the guards.

Many moons ago when things were less troubled on the reservation, when we were all young and beautiful, a royal commission in Britain into hospital auxiliary workers said, "although the work carried out by auxiliary workers in hospitals is less glamourous than that carried out by doctors, it is none the less important." It is not negotiation through manipulation or excessive greed which is a solution, but rather a level playing pitch where the rights of all are acknowledged and recognised – not just for the glamourous and chic but also the ready-to-wear types like myself.

FIVE MEDITATIONS

I

"CAN I USE the toilet?" A simple request expressed in an authentic Dublin accent somewhere in Dublin's inner city. Very often the authentic flatness of the speaker's voice betrays him, like a leper's cries of "unclean!" It reveals him as an insignificant statistic, as a member of a low-income socio-economic grouping in a government department annual report. This chronicle relates to the social deprivation which accompanies drug addiction, unemployment, alcoholism, suicide or minor criminal activity.

The answer to the person's simple and honest biological request is very often greeted with a gruff negative response, vocal tones that manifest the origins of its very serious owner's rural genealogy. The response, even if it is in the negative, does succeed in dignifying the person who asked the question with a reply, "Sorry, toilets are for customers' use only."

In the life of our Lord, would there have been social strata and bourgeois snobbery in existence, whereby somebody from Nazareth, a small town, would reveal his humble origins by the flatness of his accent to an important educated merchant from Jerusalem? Would he be subjected to prejudice and bigotry because they are outside the realm of the familiar and conventional? The merchant by displaying his disposition and nature is at ease and comfortable with his prejudices, even at the moral expense of participating in social exclusion.

There is a famous story about the American writer Gertrude Stein who on her deathbed was asked by one of her dedicated acolytes, "Gertrude, what is the answer?" Gertrude's famous reply was "What was the question?" The question still remains "Can I use the toilet?"

II

THE ART of creativity is undoubtedly a mysterious activity, Aristotle's theory of plot is helpful – beginning, middle and end. Firstly it is like a view from a window, looking out at the immediate terrain. Then, perhaps extending to the mountains on the horizon and filling the viewer with awe and wonder at what lies beyond.

The creative impulse abounds a lot in nature as well as art; in great art it definitely contains a spiritual dimension. Perhaps in our humanity both worlds can meet as at the dance at the crossroads a major event in our great grandparents' social diary in the distant past.

Perhaps people at their best are an embodiment of art and nature – the dance and the music and the moonlight and the starry sky. A great theatre which God packed an audience into to share his creation and in which he wanted people to be the stars. "What is the stars, Joxer? What is the stars?" wrote Sean O'Casey in *The Plough and the Stars*. I have an uncanny feeling that Sean O'Casey knew the answer to the question: people. How else could he have been a great dramatist if he did not know the magnetic poles of great happiness and great tragedy?

Indeed how can we know or have any chance of knowing unless like the sunrise and the sunset we need, as a rehearsal, a little death and resurrection every day of our lives.

III

AN HONEST FAILURE is better than a dishonest success. Most of us know, or maybe some more than others the kind of total collapse of morale and feeling of well-being that occurs when disaster rips our world apart. That time in our lives when a tornado of bad luck and misfortune strikes tragically, the residue being a dung heap of emotion.

A story from my school days still floats back to me as an adult with pleasant stirrings of time and nostalgia. The story is the story of Coco the Clown. The story goes, the once-very famous clown called Coco, who made people laugh till they cried, made people simply deliriously happy. Then the story continues, an old man so depressed he went from one doctor to another seeking some respite from his gloom and sadness.

So after visiting many doctors with no success, he was recommended to a very famous doctor, the most respected in his field. The doctor studied the patient's chart in front of him on his desk then he studied the look of great sadness on the old man's face. He spoke after careful consideration, "There is a very famous clown visiting the town at the moment, his name is Coco and I strongly recommend that you go and see him in the circus."

There was a frozen silence, then the old man spoke. He replied barely audibly, "I am Coco."

Life is sometimes like a circus within a circus – only a sad charade when people are not telling the truth, so misleading others with alibis and lies as well as themselves so they become very unhappy. It is only through the truth you have a chance of being happy.

The story taught me if you do not try, even if you fail miserably you will never know what it is to succeed. Perhaps there is a touch of Coco the Clown in all of us, trying to pretend on the outside that things are going well, only to be haunted by demons inside which we cannot hide from. If what Bob Dylan said is true, "There is no success like failure and failure is no success at all." So then the words of the poet John Keats are also true. "Truth is beauty, beauty is truth. This is all you need to know."

IV

WE ARE ALL exposed to danger, especially in the world we live in today. It could be an unexpected violent attack at the hands of a mugger, or the common reality of domestic violence. People should know about being the victim of violent assault. The amazing speed with which it happens, like mercury sliding snake-like in a thermometer, when the instant second might result in your death, then the experience is very frightening alive with drama and high terror. Cities are full of these alarming hellish realities, particularly late at night on badly lit streets. The hooded youths seem to appear from nowhere out of the shadows like bats moving in the dark.

The opening scene in the drama is to prevent your screams for help being heard. First there is the forceful large gloved hand placed across your mouth, then the painful twisting of your arm, then tightly shoving your arm up behind your back. A forceful push hurls you against the nearest wall, as a free accomplice reaches into your pockets hoping to find a wallet stuffed with notes. The accompanying chant falling on your ears like an evil mantra, "Where's the money, where's the money?" "I have no money." I must have been like a mugger's mugger.

The American Beat poet Lawrence Ferlinghetti has a line in one of his poems which goes, "Evil is Live spelt backwards." The implication seems to be destructive energy is energy without a loving creative outlet. So much energy misguided, if it did have creative channel then it could become loving creativity. Truth seems to bring us closer to life, lies seem to bring us away from life. Notwithstanding the words of the poet Lord Byron "what is a lie, but the truth in masquerade." In the words of Nelson Mandela "If people can learn to hate each other, then they can also learn to love each other."

V

THIS MORNING as most mornings an event or events will happen which you will participate in. You might be caught in slow-moving traffic moving so slow it is like a snail seen to be going backwards just taking its time, because he is not too pressurised by commitments and is totally uninterested in important meetings or the pressure of appointments.

Then you might be a mother feeding the baby his bottle and to your horror you see a piece of eggshell in the milk left over from the morning's breakfast and you have to start all over again. Then you realise the family dog has just chewed the last remaining nappy and you want to scream. Depressed you wonder to yourself should you sign yourself into a House for the Bewildered.

Indeed you might be waiting patiently on a bus to get to the labour exchange to sign on because through no fault of your own you are not working at the moment in these difficult economic times. Suddenly twice in quick succession the bus arrives but fails to stop as it is full up. So you are very worried that you might not receive your small amount of payment if you fail to keep your appointment.

Some days did Jesus feel like not getting out of bed at all? Some days would St Joseph have preferred not to think about the household bills and the money that he owed, also more importantly perhaps the money that was owed to him. Did Mary some days wonder quietly in desperation to herself would this day ever end? Who can say like any family or household there were not disagreements and disappointments, frowns and tears, smiles and laughter, success and failure. This poem was written at daybreak on the banks of the Grand Canal adjacent to Portobello Bridge as opposed to Baggot St Bridge where the poet Patrick Kavanagh was wont to take his ease and reflect. The poem is called "Early Morning Cantata." Here is a short extract:

> A family of innocents not afraid to be happy
> Who know so well what it is to be sad.
> The leaves on the beech tree applaud,
> Their green skins rustling on their branches,
> The crossing flights of gulls and pigeons,
> Across this restful Portobello spectacle,
> The tribe's practice to retreat to a quiet place,
> And reflect, with the guidance of birdsong.

NORTHSIDER

I

WHITWORTH ROAD, Drumcondra on the north side of Dublin, in close proximity to the city centre, is home territory for me. Tomorrow, Sunday, further down the Royal Canal, all the cheers and excitement of supporters in Croke Park will be heard. At another time it might have been the legendary sound of the Dalymount roar, emanating from Phibsboro at the Glasnevin end of the Whitworth Road.

I am again in residence on this street, just a short distance from the house my parents lived in for thirty-five years. I am in a modest bedsit, suitably strewn with notes and loosely organised manuscripts. I am near St Vincent's CBS in Glasnevin, where I attended school until fifth year, when I first responded to the call of the wild, little did I know that I would later visit the Yukon. I played truant or went on the bounce to the Botanic Gardens with a good book like *The Grapes of Wrath*, *The Man with the Golden Arm* or *The Vicar of Wakefield*.

The site of my Alma Mater is now a block of luxury flats, as is the site of Lemon's Pure Sweets factory which is now a housing complex by the River Tolka. Here too is Players cigarette factory, which I visited as a young teenager with a friend for a bazz off school to avail of the complimentary ten cigarettes which were a real prize for a Christian Brothers' student in the early Sixties. The former Players factory is now part of the Smurfit Group.

Formative years contain for most people landmarks of trauma, serenity, heartbreak and happy days of innocence and bliss. On Drumcondra Road, just below the railway bridge, is my memory of the tanned handsome smiling face with the boyish grin and brown wavy hair of John F Kennedy beginning his visit to Ireland in the summer of 1962. Then I was on the cusp of The Beatles and Stones music and the onslaught of the Sixties generation.

On Drumcondra Road, on Binn's Bridge at the beginning of Dorset Street, with long hair and the benefit of a sojourn on the West Coast of America, I greeted Richard Millhouse Nixon much less hospitably. I had had contact with Black Panther associates in the Bay area of San Francisco who had suffered deeply in the Ghettos like Marin City because of Nixon's unenlightened policies. I have also attended memorials for those who died in the Vietnam war.

As I write this late at night, the sounds of my childhood are recreated through my window in the lonely quiet of the night by the clickety-clack, shunting, then passing, of the goods train heading west. The railway line runs at the back of this abode and the former family residence.

Across the newly landscaped Royal Canal, aided by grants from local government, is the stark ominous presence of a latter-day Bastille, known for its famous list of inmates – Kevin Barry, Brendan Behan – Mountjoy Jail, a relic of colonialism.

Just off Dorset Street, on the North Circular Road, is a plaque to Sean O'Casey where the playwright wrote *Juno and the Paycock* in very modest surroundings. One of the poems of James Joyce's *Chamber Music* described a drover coming down the North Circular Road with some cattle from the cattle market, now also rebuilt as flats and houses. Joyce attended the Jesuits in Belvedere College on Denmark Street, off Parnell Square. This runs perpendicular to North Great George's Street where on Bloomsday one year, 16 June, the Minister for Finance, Bertie Ahern, TD for this area, opened the new James

Joyce Museum, long pioneered by Senator David Norris. The director of the museum is a nephew of Joyce, Ken Monahan.

Today the Dublin Writers' Museum is situated on Parnell Square. In my teens a little heartthrob from the suburbs attended a secretarial course when the museum was the site of a former technical school. At the bottom of the hill is the Rotunda Hospital, where I first saw the light.

In Charleville Tennis Club, situated at the Glasnevin end of my street, was a surging, sweating, Turkish bath of young people discovering rock 'n' roll and "lurching," as this form of slow dance was aptly called. This was a long way from waltzing and the courteous, self-disciplined care of a calculated movement with order and decorum – more a full-blooded, passionate embrace, clutching the female with sweaty palms and perspiration in tidal waves flowing down the forehead. This prompted one young lady to say to her partner, a young Don Juan, "I think you should leave room for the Holy Spirit to breathe."

The Church of St Columbus on Iona Road, which still houses in its ground a primary school and the infants school which I attended in a flood of tears on my first day in the halls of learning. I used to cross and re-cross the old red iron bridge like a snail or a tortoise afraid of the possibility of the wonders of modern technology.

Somewhere in my travels I heard a story about Iona Road and the Black and Tans. Some poor innocent, who was about to be arrested in a round-up by these gents, was asked: "Where do you live, mate?"

"Iona Road."

The Tan's reply was "I don't care what you own, you are still coming in for questioning."

Obviously it is not where *his* sensibilities began.

II

I WILL ALWAYS remember my first day at school. It could have been raining – well it might as well have been raining because I shed such a shower of tears.

September 1950, aged four years and 10 months, baby infants Saint Columbus School, Iona Road. I didn't think this was a great career move, so I reacted accordingly.

But there were happy times, chasing a small blue ball around the schoolyard with my classmates during the break. However, best of all, there always came the glorious ring of the bell and the sacred hour of going home.

We climbed, my companions and I, the red iron railway bridge that still links Lindsay Road and Claude Road. I lived on nearby Whitworth Road between Claude Road and Wigan Road.

On the way home from school there was the competition – whose school bag could be thrown the greatest distance from the landing of the red iron bridge. The journey home from school was definitely a lot more fun than the nine o'clock start on a cold winter's morning.

I remember the tall formidable nun with the high white collar, and rosary beads, with a long leather strap dangling from her hip, like a high powered weapon with which she kept law and order in the classroom of potential juvenile delinquents.

At home, the radio was the main event in the evening. The crackling wireless in 1956 from the BBC World Service announced the Russian crackdown in Hungary. In Slavic Hungarian broken English, the voice came over the radio: "What is the United Nations doing? What is the Free World doing?"

From Radio Éireann there was the Sunday night play from the Radio Éireann repertory players, *The Kennedys of Castleross* and the topical talk after the news at one-thirty lunchtime.

From the BBC, there was *Mrs Dale's Diary* and the doctor's wife's famous line: "I'm a bit worried about Jim." Paddy Crosbie's *School Around the Corner* and most importantly "The Funny Incident".

I remember a major news story from America which made the headline – would Carol Chessman, who had success as a best selling author, get a reprieve from the electric chair? The drama was a major talking point to and from school – the result was the chair was plugged in.

Memorable sounds of childhood were the clip-clopping of the horses from Merville Dairies, which had its headquarters on Finglas Road. The horses' hooves of the baker, Johnston Mooney and O'Brien, also provided an equine musical kind of calypso at lunchtime.

The sight of the first swallows was a great moment and the arrival of the swans on the Royal Canal between Cross Guns Bridge and Binn's Bridge. These signals meant that summer was on the way.

Then there was football and more football, the child's declaration of freedom, the days of summer that you hoped would never end.

As primary school came to a close, the experience of the regime was too much for some of my fellow students. For others St Mary's Rathmines beckoned, Belvedere College for others and for yet others, boarding school. Anything for a better life.

The first phone call I was ever allowed to make, 6 February, 1958, was to tell my friend about the Munich air disaster – the famous air crash where many of Matt Busby's babes perished.

It included Liam Whelan from Cabra, Duncan Edwards, Roger Byrne and the centre-forward Tommy Taylor. A dark cloud of grief hovered over the Northside of Dublin for a long time after the death of Liam Whelan.

Soccer was the staple diet of schoolboy life on the Northside and still is. I had a happy, if brief, career as a half back with Stella Maris on Richmond Road. Part of my peer group included Terry Conroy, later an Irish international who played for Home Farm, and Eoin Hand who played on the under 17s while I played under 16s.

There was Jimmy Conway who played for Fulham and the Republic of Ireland. On an ideal space, opposite Drumcondra Football Club on Richmond Road, on idyllic sunny evenings in April and May, Eamon Dunphy – on holidays from Millwall – joined in.

The budding poet in me led me to seek out solitude and isolation. There were many reflective pleasant hours spent in a quiet spot, high up on Howth Head observing the whirls, glides and dives of the seagulls and the birds of the air. To watch the boats in Dublin Bay on their bobbing little sea journeys gave me great solace.

The River Tolka I found a source of great inspiration, at high flow in Tolka Park in winter. It could have been Niagara Falls. It was my Mississippi River, the Danube, the Amazon, the Yangtse, the Volga, the Zambezi and the Nile. As it flowed it was all life, all time, all hopes I had, all dreams. I was part of it so it belonged to me as much as anybody else. It seemed to say to me that it cared about me and all the people who knew it acknowledged its very special place in the scheme of things.

It was a kind of God to me. It was above reproach and criticism, it was like a vein or an artery or a blood vessel of everybody, young and old, who lived close to it. It was my special friend because it knew me deeply and seemed to understand me.

It brought great peace to my very difficult troubled thoughts. It was inclusive not exclusive. It was on a free-wheeling, free rolling, rolling rhythm to greatness and destiny and it invited me to join in.

It seemed to say "come abroad," a jaunty roller-coaster of humanity, a simple invitation to live with no strings attached.

POOR COLD AND HOMELESS

I

WHAT IT IS LIKE TO BE HOMELESS

THE CITY of London offers attractive opportunities for advancement to young people from Ireland and the provinces of Britain and Scotland. But what appears to be the recipe for a dream come true often turns into a nightmarish reality of destitution, deprivation and homelessness.

The files of social workers, probation officers, and those in the caring professions all bear testament to this. Writing as one who fell into the social abyss of homelessness without any safety net to break the fall, I too can provide some details of the experience in London and Dublin.

One of the first things you notice about homelessness is hunger. The general consensus is that the worst pangs of hunger take place during the initial three or four days. After this time the body's system can acclimatise itself by way of adapting to the reduced nutrition. But the initial shortage of food during those three or four days is a painful process with which to cope, as the lining of the stomach contracts causing pain.

But obviously this knowledge cannot be easily explained to an irate restaurant manager, suspicious policeman or middle-class magistrate or uppercrust judge who have never been short of a meal in their lives.

The uprooted homeless person from Dublin or wherever, trying to forage for survival in London, learns as a matter of necessity to cope with suicidal feelings, like *Should I throw myself under the approaching Tube train?*

The ensuing feelings of alienation, loneliness, sense of failure, insecurity, helplessness and often anger creates the faceless and unidentifiable monster which has caused this hell of circumstance of physical and mental torture.

Human life does not necessarily have a happy ending, unlike children's fairytales. If a person is hanging on desperately to the rim of survival, the area of choice is extremely limited. The situation might be as it was for me on one occasion when I was penniless, wet and hungry in Leicester Square with no prospect of accommodation for the night. Such realities teach a homeless person to think very fast and make quick decisions.

I was surrounded by the best dining facilities which Western civilisation has to offer, which if you have money are only a few footsteps away. But if one is to confront the social conventions, or flaunt the rules of acceptable behaviour of the world of free enterprise, the penalties are often swift and severe.

A neon-lit sign outside this well-known London eatery announced the BEST CURRY IN LONDON. I took them at their word. I had the meal and would worry about the consequences later. And so I was nicked. But to solve my immediate accommodation problems, I got a bed for the night (even if it was in a police station), free transport in a paddy wagon, breakfast the following morning and the Probation Act in court.

The situation of the homeless person seeking a taste of justice is rather like a haemophiliac trying to negotiate a truce with a shoal of piranha fish – and that applies as much to Dublin as anywhere.

The Morning Star, The Iveagh Hostel, The Model Lodging House, the police cells at Pearse Street, floors, hall-ways of friends' houses set out in flats, these have all been my home. The nooks and crannies of the city became known to me, its hidden recesses, where only a few enter an unexplored world.

The citizens carry little in the way of official identity like bank books or drivers' licences, because they own nothing. Here is a sad twilight of the forgotten where the embers of memory are stirred to happier days.

I had some friends and acquaintances walking the same tightrope of survival of homelessness. Some died, like Allen found dead in a shower in Trinity College where he was one time a medical student. Jimmy was found dead from a drug overdose in a laneway off Berkeley Road. Pat died with a beatific smile on his face, addicted to the drugs which his psychiatrist prescribed for him. I heard him described by one person who knew him as a wayward genius. He was.

The world of homelessness is largely an uncharted region without maps or compasses. The main guidance system lies within the individual himself. Primitive gut instinct of a primordial nature helps him to stay alive and overcome all hazards and vicissitudes in the ordeal of daily struggle.

Such physical problems as lice, or scabies, which are acquired from being unwashed and having frequent contact with dirt and squalor. They are a normal part of the homeless person's odyssey.

In my experience, the agencies and individuals who supposedly exist to alleviate the plight of the homeless have an attitudinal problem which handicaps some well-intentioned individuals in their efforts to help. Because such individuals have little or no frame of reference to readily understand the dilemma of their homeless charges, it leaves the homeless person out on his own.

The sinking, sliding sensation of descent into a swamp from which there is no return is akin to my feelings of losing myself without the support of a base. I experienced this certainly in the West End of London. Only the homeless know this feeling, but government agencies do not share such enlightenment.

If there is one book which anybody wishing to understand should read, it is *No Fixed Abode* by Anton Wallach Clifford (published by MacMillan), a saintly man who dedicated much of his life to the plight of the homeless, founder of the Simon Community, and a great personal friend.

II

HOMELESSNESS AND THE LAW

SOMETIMES the most stable environment the homeless person finds is being in prison for a crime related to homelessness such as begging, shop-lifting because of hunger, breaking and entering because he has to forcibly break into a house for accommodation, trespassing in a park or public place, "loitering with intent," "drunk and disorderly" – which are but manifestations of the frustration, the tangle of complex and repressed emotions, that mark the plight of homelessness.

The property owner is protected by the law in the defence of his possessions; there exists a hierarchy, a network of carefully managed defence systems in the small print of innumerable legal documents for this purpose.

The entire legalistic mechanics of the judicial system dictates against the rights of the dispossessed homeless person, whereas for the educated citizen or the citizen who is a home owner or a person of modest means and property, the right to freedom or civil rights can be articulated and expressed with sophisticated argument leading to financial compensation under the law. But most importantly the individual in this category can have a sense of self-esteem and self-respect through the accruing value which the national conscience in the form of the courts and its officers of solicitors, barristers, judges and legions of assistants participate in, to redress an infringement of freedom in a dignified manner. Homeless people very often have their condition of faltering self-confidence and wavering self-esteem worsened in their contact with the law.

In the face of ruthless, severe and unjust treatment by society's pillars of justice and respectability, the situation of the homeless person seeking a taste of justice is a monumental exercise, and very often is trying to achieve the impossible.

At one time in human history, Christians were easily identifiable to the Roman soldiers who guarded them, by the way they cared about each other. The wheel of history has turned on its axis. Now perhaps it is true that the people who are closest to the real tenets of Christianity are the dispossessed homeless people on the periphery of a society in which they are outcasts. The difference between Ireland and Rome is that in Rome if the Christians were identifiable because they loved and cared deeply about each other, now the so-called Christians are obvious by the intensity of their hatred and loathing for each other.

There is within the scheme of the homeless culture – and at its deepest level – many clues for its adversaries on the other side of the river of imperialism in which the non-homeless are in greedy danger of being drowned.

The human being through love, even if it is found through squalor, poverty, deprivation and degradation, can come to know and understand another person's pain and unselfishly lend assistance in a way that is ennobling and enriching for the entire species. Is this not the thinking of some psychoanalysts who recommend to their wealthy, lonely and bored patients that they should participate in some social work to rejuvenate the tired and insensitive morality of a dead Christianity?

Sir Thomas More in *Utopia* said, "What society has to do with the criminal is to remove the reasons why he is obliged to commit crime in the first place." This logic applied to the homeless person is to remove the reasons why people become homeless and consequently get into difficulty with the law. The quality of a society is the compassion that it demonstrates towards its floundering members and so achieve an equality in society generally.

Under the legal code as it obtains in Britain and Ireland, with its prejudicial historic vendetta towards the peasant, vagrant or Paddy, the scales of justice, as they exist, are obviously not balanced equitably towards a fair deal for the homeless.

Those who make the laws tend to consider the merit of those laws for their own comfort and that of their friends and family. A home in the real sense, it may be true – according to the German author Herman Hesse – "lies at the crossroads of the human heart." But that poetic feeling is more accessible when the body is not desperately fighting the elements in search of shelter.

The focus of the dilemma quite often appears to be that the greater the efforts that the victim makes to improve his or her position, the greater the sense of frustration when meeting brick walls and cul-de-sacs.

The victims of homelessness do not choose their situation any more than another twist of fate would cause another citizen to make a voluntary choice to become terminally ill.

For all the people in cities who sleep rough and go without food and shelter there is a surfeit of comfort for many others, who if they had any will or desire could solve the problem. Homelessness is in many ways a sick situation but it is only a barometer of a society which is itself very sick.

III

SYMPATHY WITH THE POOR CAN BE JUST A LITTLE BIT RICH

FOR THOSE who suffer from what Scott Fitzgerald called "the hothouse struggles of the poor," nothing can be as discouraging to an already burdened spirit as comments like "Cheer up, it may never happen," "Smile, give your face a holiday," "Pull yourself together" or "Thank God you're alive."

All these clichés in themselves can make wonderful sense and contain some small particles of wisdom, mostly for the person who is uttering them who invariably enjoys a solid and secure dug-out of comfort and agreeability.

If the rent is not paid and the landlord is waxing lyrical about the arrears, then you know that all the clichés of social workers, concerned relatives and assistant bank managers (anyone who could perform the miracle of providing you with a few quid) will not solve your problem.

Denizens of the First World without a home have intricate knowledge of your all too real Third World dilemma, i.e. a walkabout in the rain with legions of homeless people in the modern city.

Yet people without homes actually become more advanced, not in the domain of bourgeois mod cons and Jacuzzi luxury, but in the preserve of ingenuity, tenacity and perseverance.

Tenants evicted because of failure to pay their rent are not expected to donate their organs to the landlord, while they seek out new living quarters. Nor indeed is the state expected to intervene to declare that their troubled lives should be a worry-free zone, exempt from trials and tribulations.

There are more people in the world, but there are an awful lot of houses without anybody living in them. Some houses are over-crowded, others are empty.

Part of the reason must be that there is no such species as a landlord who gives the rent back to the tenant after it is paid, just in case the tenant might want to save up and put a down payment on a house of his or her own. Our civilisation has not yet evolved that far.

How would the monkeys in the jungle feel if they had to pay a rent to Tarzan for an ordinary monkey bedsit in a banana tree? They would say to themselves this is not good monkey business, particularly since some of the other monkeys have a better view of the mountain, for the same price up the same tree and they are closer to the best bananas. Tarzan would have a lot to answer for; he might have a monkey revolution on his hands.

Imagine the monkeys negotiating hot and heavy with Tarzan culminating in Tarzan having to pay rent to the monkeys, because the monkeys were in the jungle before Tarzan. Tarzan, they declare, is only a squatter.

If Tarzan wants security of tenure, he has to apply to the council of monkeys, like all other squatters, for full monkey approval. Furthermore he will have to pay rent to the council of monkeys. This is good monkey business.

I am cheering on the monkeys.

IV

A PLACE TO CALL YOUR OWN

RAFTERY the poet knew more than most about the occupational hazards of the no-fixed abode literary journeyman and wandering bard. "Now spring is coming, and after the feast day of St Brigid, I will be in the heart of Co Mayo."

Even the Gospels record the angst of the lord. "The birds of the air have their nests, the foxes have their lairs, but the son of man has no place to lay his head." But for a lot of people, the signpost to that destination can appear deceptive and misleading, even impossible to locate.

Many people nowadays echo the sentiments of Padraic Colum's poem "The Old Woman Of The Road," "Oh to have a little house." Particularly one with the mortgage paid for and the children's way paid through college and the medical bills taken care of. In America, the land that created the travelling hobo on the freight trains in the Thirties, their dispossessed spokesperson was Woody Guthrie, the forerunner of Bob Dylan and the modern singer-songwriter. His favourite song was the hobo's lullaby. "Go to sleep you weary hobo/Let the towns drift slowly by/Raise your head and smile at trouble/You'll find peace and rest some day."

What children and young teenagers accept with blind faith and unquestioningly, board and lodging and a modicum of creature comforts, sometimes surfaces as the dream of an engaged or newly-married couple or an unmarried mother. They transpire to be as elusive as the Yeti in the Himalayas, which a hunter is trying to capture, but who by an uncanny twist of fate becomes the hunted.

The carefully made plans and schemes to acquire the great prize of a house, or a reasonable dwelling, become the nightmare and hell of a hostel, homelessness, prison, a mental hospital or a battered wives' refuge. Between the ceiling of what once was a high dream, and the floor of a bumpy reality is all the heartbreak of modern distress.

Housing has long been a festering sore in the body of the national politic, with little medicine or government care. The "doctor," the government, does not understand the "patients'" symptoms. They are, for those seeking a roof over their heads: no security of tenure, acute financial insecurity, constant and severe exploitative tactics by landlords. They prey on the weak and vulnerable who are not protected by a clearly-defined charter of rights as also obtains with the mentally ill and unstable.

Students know more than most sections of the community about the small corner of solitude and privacy necessary to develop their intellectual skills and talents in the context and setting of a reasonable budget and facilities. But, similarly, the talents of children and any wholesome gifted person endeavouring to pursue their life's path also deeply need a life setting that is people-friendly and has a human face.

When the 1916 leaders were drafting the proclamation, the idea of nationhood contained, in this cornerstone of vision homes and domesticity for the people. The American constitution contains the proviso for the right of people to pursue happiness as part of their birthright. But to imply that this can be done without a roof over one's head is like saying it's possible to breathe without having lungs.

The role models for a lot of the governments of the world were ancient Greece and Rome and their august senators political and philosophical doyens. But these lofty intellects had their Roman villas, Roman baths, Roman coins and slaves to support their political and cultural designs. The Barbarians outside the Roman and Greek pale did not.

Perhaps a timely and opportune innovation for the modern dispossessed might be an increased awareness of their needs and culture. A government agency to log, tabulate, research and assess what is needed for those in a gladiatorial struggle in the coliseum of the second millennium, where no prisoners are taken, and the lions are more ravenous and vicious than ever. Even if your simple purpose is seeking a place to call your own.

LONDON ENCOUNTERS

I

ALCOHOL is an equaliser. But it depends on who you are drinking with: a bully, a liar, a fraudster – or if you are being the recipient of the courtesy, gentleness and charm of a world-famous playwright.

London can be such an interesting city but, oh, so lonely! As in all cities, there is heartbreak and tragedy just below the innocuous, glitzy, unassuming surface. To spend time there is to taste the flavours of its orchards: they might be bitter or they might be sweet.

My game plan, back in the 1970s, was to try and get a book of poems published, even if it took miraculous intervention. A publisher's tale, which I had heard explained to me many times, was that poetry lists were very short and books were planned about two years in advance. Anyway, poetry did not sell, and, most importantly, did not make money.

Behind the bar

While in London I had the problem of keeping body and soul together and earning a living. I knew from previous experiences in the hallowed court of St James that a job as a barman was a desirable prize, providing food and accommodation and a little money. I worked behind the bar of the Irish Club in Eaton Square, the Cadogan on the King's Road, Chelsea, the North Pole Bar adjacent to White City, a hostelry in the borough of Hendon opposite the Police Academy, and the Mayflower in Rotherhithe with an idyllic view of the River Thames.

As time passed I had a succession of other jobs: dishwasher-cum-kitchen porter in the Café Royale, a job in the culinary care department of Springfield Mental Hospital, cleaner-cum-messenger with British Rail, and road-sweeper with Westminster City Council.

In the meantime, I made some progress towards getting the book of poems published through the good offices of the director of the National Poetry Society in Earls Court. I showed a brief recommendation of my work by the poet and professor Brendan Kennelly to the society's director. At the time I was without a job; then received a double week's holiday social security payment. My problem was solved; I could now afford the publishing costs.

While in the vicinity of Chalk Farm one night, desperate for a bed, it was Anton Wallach Clifford, being a lover of the arts and a benefactor of the homeless who provided a settee for a month while I organised my publishing project. He also, through his many contacts, arranged an early morning interview on BBC Radio London to a million listeners and a press conference; such was the generosity of the man. Soon after, the great day arrived when my book of poems was launched at the London headquarters of the Simon Community on Maldon Road, Chalk Farm.

It was not until a long time after that I learned the words of wisdom of Herman Melville, author of *Moby Dick*: "There is nothing less consequential in literature than the publication of a first book of poems." I was temporarily spared the truth. The book was out. A short time later my tax rebate cheque also arrived.

New-found wealth

On the way home one evening I ventured into the Roundhouse for Performing Arts. There was a Tennessee Williams play on that night. In the bar I ordered a drink with my new-found wealth from the Revenue. Then I noticed a bespectacled, moustached man of average height, dressed in a dark-brown khaki jacket. It struck me that he might be Tennessee Williams, as I had read his article in *The Times* the previous morning. There was one way to find out. "Are you Tennessee Williams?" I asked.

"I am," replied the friendly southern gent.

"Can I buy you a drink?" I said.

"No thanks, I have one, but I will join you in a moment."

After we had talked a little I commented on his article in *The Times*, which had told me something about his life and the variety of jobs he had done. "You describe them as 'all good jobs,'" I said. I had been amazed, thinking of myself pushing my brushes and cart through snowy streets in winter, the endless bottles which I had to put one by one in crates in the Irish pubs in which I had worked, not to mention the work as a kitchen porter in Soho. "All good jobs," he happily volunteered, through a toothy, charming smile.

A low ebb

I mentioned to him the bits of writing I'd been engaged in; then I volunteered a poem which somewhat reflected my angst while at a low ebb in the not-too-distant past. The poem was entitled "I'm sorry I cannot help you."

> You are homeless and have nowhere to live, I'm sorry I cannot help you.
> You are suicidal and may kill yourself, I'm sorry I cannot help you.
> You are on drugs and feel very upset, I'm sorry I cannot help you.
> You are so alone, you are aloneness itself, I'm sorry I cannot help you.
> I'm selfish and I keep extremely busy to cope with my loneliness.
> I'm sorry I cannot help you.

At this point Tennessee Williams interjected in his slow affable accent: "That's a mighty fine line." At the end of the poem he said: "That's a good one."

For me, meeting him was a benign signpost from a literary giant to a pilgrim on the road looking for directions. The play that was showing in the Roundhouse was *The Red Devil Battery Sign* – a later work, not an early classic like *A Streetcar Named Desire, Cat on a Hot Tin Roof*, *The Glass Menagerie*, *Suddenly Last Summer*, *Sweet Bird of Youth*, or *Night of the Iguana*. As he was about to take his leave, I said, "You must visit Dublin."

He replied, again smiling broadly, "I must go everywhere."

II

STAYING WITH ANTON

IT WAS ON a rain-sodden, windswept, winter's night in the London borough of Kentish town that I first met Anton Wallich Clifford, the founder of the Simon Community, who died 25 years ago on 30 July, 1978.

The address of the Simon house on Maldon Road, in the adjacent borough of Chalk Farm, was provided by a kindly padre. It gave me hope in a hopeless situation. London is at its grimmest when you are cold, wet, hungry, penniless and homeless. I was carrying a suitcase with all my worldly possessions. I felt like a character in Ralph McTell's song, popular at the time, "The Streets of London," whom Ralph had omitted to mention in his roll-call of London's misfits. I was part of the desperate army of night-walkers who just barely managed to survive by taking one step at a time in the uncharted world of the homeless. I knew I was on a very slippery slope.

On entering the house of hospitality, as Anton fondly christened his oasis of refuge, I knew instinctively by his striking humanity and aura of gentleness that this was a very special man, and as time passed and I got to know him better I found out why. I was offered accommodation on a settee for the time it took to organise publishing my first book of poetry at the National Poetry Society in Earls Court Square. At the end of the daily efforts there was always a hot meal and a welcome rest.

The residents of the house on Maldon Road were an assortment of fascinating people. There was a frail Englishman, possibly from

Manchester, with an angular, smallish, bird-like head and torso. There was an 18-year-old Turkish student, with a big bush of black curly hair and eyes like raspberries, who was more or less impossible to understand. Anton suggested that I might be able to help him with his English. There was Cyril, a classic study of a senior citizen always about to get fully out of his depth but not quite doing so. I saw him totally flummox a recent social work graduate more familiar with textbooks than people when she was reluctant to provide him with his ration of snout – cigarettes to you. Cyril simply said, "For Christ's sake I can't survive without them. Give me the bleedin' cigarettes."

There was the weather-beaten former Icelandic trawler captain who never lost his toughness and grit to survive even when the high seas of the Arctic Ocean were replaced by the waves of poverty. Then there was Lynn, a blonde, attractive girl in her mid-twenties who knew her way unescorted around the West End, maybe too well for her own good. The house was not without little moments of rancour and in such a small space tempers sometimes flared. There were also moments of passion and crisis. But at the centre was Anton the pragmatist, the businessman and the serene saint, at times ruffled and beleaguered by the effort to make ends meet. There were workers and volunteers who did not always come up to scratch and expectation. There were disappointments – many of them; but there was also the support of many loyal friends and admirers. And there was also success – perhaps an outreach to a badly neglected group of meths drinkers.

On occasion, caught in the glue works of my own problems, I escorted Anton on his daily visits to Mass. These were to me quite inspirational moments. During the sign of peace in the Mass Anton seemed to arrive at a plateau of fulfilment, such was the warmth of his regard for his fellow travellers. Late at night at peace after the workload of another day, when we sometimes quietly chatted, he showed a very lively sense of humour, a most necessary piece of equipment to survive in the face of struggle and adversity. With pipe in mouth, he resembled a bespectacled Indian chief, puffing smoke to heaven and sometimes serenely smiling. He explained to me how the idea of the Simon Community germinated in his mind. After he was demobbed from the RAF where he served during the war he worked as a probation officer in Bow Street magistrates court in London. After the week's work and looking after his charges he would retire to have a pint with the landlord of a nearby hostelry.

From the landlord's office he could see the customers he looked after on a daily basis in his office. They were all, to varying degrees, in dire straits of desperation, moving from one crisis to the next, and always looking for a bed for the night, thanks to the makeshift facilities offered by the Department of Social Security and its allies in housing welfare agencies. He saw a chance to make a difference, to gain respite for these lives jammed between the devil and the deep abyss of no-man's-land.

Anton worked, cared and suffered for prostitutes, drug addicts, ex-convicts, pimps and all those who were burdened; and he loved them all. The last time I saw him was when he came to see me while visiting Dublin late in 1977. On occasions we would talk on the phone. His death after a short illness came as such a shock. But what a great and glorious thing he achieved when with simple faith and integrity he succeeded in lifting the burden of the homeless and heroically lightening their load.

WRITING AND WRITERS

A WEEK IN THE LIFE OF A WRITER

"YOU CAN'T do it when you are worried about something." This applies to many things, and it was some of the valuable advice given by John McGahern, whom I admire greatly, at a Writers' Workshop under the auspices of the Arts Council at Galway University some 15 years ago.

Worry takes many forms and plays havoc on the vulnerable and exploitable. It can disguise itself in the secretive sinister garb of an intellectual bully or mental thug; and they certainly abound nowadays. The pattern of some worries, if the last week is a clue, seems to lead a life of its own; then it dies an inglorious death. But before it does, it reaches a crescendo of frustration, anger that just avoids exploding, panic that is controlled by a strong sense of hope.

Then there is anxiety for the future which seems to be calmed by incautious but generous optimism, and most of all a sense of humour that defies tragedy and disaster. Perhaps this creature surfacing from the bowels of experience goes by the name of maturity, or it could be another disguise of my old friend self-deception.

Grants for literary projects such as my drama one are difficult to procure: money is not as freely available as the falling autumnal leaves that can be swept into neat bundles of disposable greenbacks. "It is only those who attempt the absurd can achieve the impossible" – so said Robert Kennedy in Kennedy Square in Detroit shortly before his assassination in

May 1968. Originally, as the senator from Massachusetts pointed out, it was one of the quotable quotes of George Bernard Shaw.

This is the season of the theatre, with the cortège of thespian-worshippers lined up in a long queue of sacramental devotion outside Read's agreeable pub on Dame Street, Dublin 2. They are parched with an artistic search for a drink, and self-congratulatory props to their fragile insecurities and rather large oversized egos, sometimes richly deserved but not the unearned inherited right of the arrogant. This species densely populates the corridors of all art, but particularly the theatre with its own skeletal secrets, well endowed with corpses in its graveyard of lost and buried ambitions.

On Monday I met a fellow traveller in the Dublin branch of the literary trade who was somewhat short in the cash-flow. He cost me a small donation from my rent allowance; but he is also a dear friend. The waiting in the local Health Centre was alleviated somewhat by retiring on some pretext to a nearby place of business for a cup of coffee. Then – to a suitable rebuke from the attendant – I resumed my place in the queue, which had dwindled to a minimum quota an hour and a half later.

The world of publishing, into which I have previous brief forays, can be, as Charles Dickens said, "the best of times and the worst of times." Small capital makes it a highly perilous enterprise, and very much a do-it-yourself kit of self-taught techniques; the knowledge is arrived at through errors and *faux pas*.

Armed now with a computer and printer (even if they are in Galway) I might have three books on the market for Christmas or thereabouts. After all, miracles are possible.

Amnesia has fogged my mind about Tuesday, this also being the hunting season for flats by students returning to college, seeking a modicum of independence from parental pressure and domestic bonds that they desperately want to sever. The big problem is filthy lucre, trying to generate the deposit. A young scholar I met on Wednesday morning fortunately succeeded in so doing: it was provided by a benevolent brother!

She was a self-confessed problem child, but mild conjecture suggests, as Paddy Kavanagh was wont to opine, "no problem is so great that a handful of fivers won't solve it."

The drama project referred to is now with the Arts Council, a collaboration involving five artists, an innovative and exciting idea, I'm sure of it. The pain of waiting for a decision and its verdict I will know this coming Friday. A lot of work went into its development to the present stage; under-confidence might possibly cushion the blow of rejection.

Prior to the opening of the Dublin Theatre Festival I enjoyed my visit to the Gate Theatre and Brian Friel's *Molly Sweeney* with its excellent cast. It includes TP McKenna whom I have admired for a long time, and I had the pleasure of meeting Catherine Byrne (Molly) who, within a long litany of achievement, was most notable, for me, in Tom Murphy's *Whistle in the Dark*. Mark Lambert plays a most engaging bumptious character who cleverly probes the Irish male psyche. The entire play explores the hidden recesses of a troubled nation only partially sighted, through the eyes of a blind woman.

Walking down Dorset Street late on Friday night (not everybody's chosen exercise time), I noticed the name of the play showing in the Olympia Theatre: *The Street of Crocodiles.* It seemed so apt.

The news that gave me most joy during the week was the Loyalist ceasefire. Maybe now, after what so long seemed like an irreversible unending nightmare, there is a glimpse of a dream that can really come true.

Sunday morning and the gulls perform acrobatics, aerial somersaults like flying dancers on the canal, a beautiful sight.

A DAY IN THE LIFE OF A WRITER

THE DAY began at 7.30am with melodious and soothing music from the repertoire of Radio One. Autumn "of mists and mellow fruitfulness" à la Keats, Friday towards the end of November, special as it precedes my Sagittarian birthday by a few days.

Life runs along and waits for neither fools nor writers. Today being rent day, my responsibilities are deeply embedded in my brain. No rent. The streets beckon, cold and uninviting in this prelude to the bitter cold of winter.

One of the features of the changing landscape of my native city is the new and varied choice of venue available for breakfast, ever rippling towards the nest of Dubliners from the ever guileful ocean of free enterprise.

The radio in its litany of the weekend social calendar has announced the Patrick Kavanagh Weekend in the poet's native Monaghan. One is left to wonder what the bard of Inniskeen would make of the well-heeled culture vultures flocking to his birthplace to honour him while in his lifetime he received little support.

A good breakfast, the most important meal of the day, is reasonable medical advice. After which the problem of the soldier without his gun in Phibsboro is less of an intellectual teaser than a poet without food. The point being, the soldier also needs sustenance to hold his gun, if he has a gun to hold, God forbid even if it is to shoot the poet.

From the morning paper I have gleaned news of Paul Hill's future life in America with his radiant bride. Perhaps the release of the Guildford Four may be the happy augury for the less well represented Irish legal cases in the British Courts.

I have a hospital appointment. The waiting involved tempts me to turn to verse on the subject. There is a blackboard with a piece of chalk, but as my thoughts begin to bubble the geological quill refuses to co-operate. My profundity is only marginal, "waiting is sent to test our mettle/But I am being badly stung by this man-made nettle."

There is also an appointment with my Community Welfare Office about my rent allowance. So I attempt bi-location by leaving the world of medicine, only to return later, for the sake of the filthy lucre which I badly need. The interview, although the CWO is recent to the ranks of rent patronage for the masses, is very thorough.

The questions test all the recesses of my cranium and involve a lot of checking and re-checking. I leave, with largesse, a much favoured altar of the God who presides over those who wait.

In the bowels of the city I meet a very dear friend who has slipped from the pinnacle of the cattle trade to difficult and dire straits. We retire from the Theatre of War for a discussion about our mutual welfare. In my mind I am acutely aware of the need to redeem the typewriter from the pawnshop. Also the rent still has to be paid.

I go and redeem the typewriter from "the Uncle's" and head home to balance the overdue rent. A rejection slip from a newspaper awaits me, but already I have a plan to use the piece in a radio talk show. A song which I entered into a competition requires duplication so I go to the studio to get the tapes. The young lady is nice and explains how busy they are at weekends. The traffic is heavy as I go across the Matt Talbot Bridge to deliver the tapes for recording.

I have a strong urge to flee the world of heavy traffic so as to avoid the sensibilities' delicate nerve-endings being totally annihilated by the rigours of late 20th century technology, even if it is only for a weekend.

As I pass Bus Áras the large chariots are leaving for the country. I look in their direction, enviously, and think of the peace of Donegal or the tranquillity of Connemara.

Around the city there is evidence of the forthcoming mayhem of Christmas: the seasonal mass hysteria is at hand. Cliff Richard is on the Late Late Show singing his Christmas hit of last year. In the pub close to the Werburgh Labour Exchange he receives a warm reception. "He's better than Elvis," says one pint-swilling critic. "Would you get outta that," says another.

He sings "Bachelor Boy" and a flood of memories are brought back. Earlier in the evening in some of the Yuppie pubs around Mount Street, I was reminded of the words of wisdom of a former professor; "The sharks on the land are more dangerous than those at sea. Also poison sometimes takes a highly innocuous dangerous disguise."

I meet a friend, a local historian who, like myself, encounters all the vicissitudes of a freelancer's way of life. He discusses his possible whereabouts for the main event of the Christian calendar. After a few maybes and buts, he finally says that he may select the solitude option.

Passing down Dame Street later, around midnight, the lights of the Olympia Theatre are flickering alluringly. This was, once upon a time, my workplace when Richard

Condron of Norwich Playhouse fame gave me a job. I was just out of school and there was a vacancy for my friend and I. We ignited the smoke fuse when the genie appeared on stage in *Aladdin*. It starred Jack Cruise, Patricia Cahill, Ronnie Walsh and Chris Curran.

Times change. Tonight's headliners at Midnight at the Olympia are Pete Cummins and the Fleadh Cowboys. I don't believe that there are any better interpreters of Bob Dylan songs. I first heard them when they gigged on Sunday afternoons in the Lower Deck in Portobello Harbour.

However, I join the queue for Bad Bob's Backstage Bar, where the cover charge includes a curry. Eating and drinking seem to make strange bed-fellows around the city. We could take a leaf out of our European neighbours' book of etiquette; maybe, as we advance further down the European road, worthwhile changes will occur.

In this Mecca of Country and Western music are many key witnesses to the fact that a lot of Dubliners do not want to go straight home after the pubs close. In spite of the crowd, and Sandy Kelly singing in the background, I enter a civilised conversation about existentialism. Security here is tight, but the conversation is good as I sympathise with the young man working for Córas Trachtála who is having difficulty reading Sartre's novel *Nausea*.

I stop at the all-night shop on Dorset Street to get some provisions – basics such as coal, milk, bread, coffee. So I do a little accountancy. As I pay off the taxi driver in Phibsboro, I explain that I am like a man crossing Niagara on a tightrope in a heavy gale without a balancing pole. There you go.

A WRITER'S PROBLEM

ACCORDING to Virginia Woolf, the first acquisition that a writer needs is a room of one's own. Perhaps an understanding of this profound truth is only arrived at through not having a room. Whether this stems from family overcrowding, as in my own case, or the very rough justice of homelessness in the modern city, both are acute and emotionally disturbing thorns.

Maslow's theory of the hierarchy of needs, based on food and shelter, might most of all apply to this artist, since he or she, by the nature of the work of a cerebral nature, needs food, sleep, sustenance, and a modicum of creature comforts.

I live in the centre of a capital city, where problems, not only for myself, but for many people abound. In company with my fellow citizens I am of course more interested in solutions, rather than the ever-expanding complexities of entanglements.

Approximately thirty-four years ago I had a psychotic breakdown on LSD, then fashionably accessible and popular. I was twenty-three years of age.

One of the diagnoses was that my condition was drug-induced schizophrenia. As one who spent a number of years in California in the late Sixties, the tag does not faze, embarrass or otherwise astound me.

"There is none so pure as a reformed whore," goes the old wives' tale. I am more a sexual athlete who is just not endowed with the former physical vigour of my early youth. I am not a hurler on the ditch, but I am holding on to my mental energies like an alcoholic to the price of his next drink.

My addiction now is a few pints of Guinness, a hit of nicotine and caffeine. Gone are the old foggy clouds of marijuana and hashish, that shrouded San Francisco and Los Angeles in the early morning mist and smog.

A number of very fine writers have wrestled with the beasts of drink and drugs. Some went on to write masterpieces using their own experiences as the vehicle to mobilise their dilemmas, and sublimated them through the creative imagination into art-books such as *Junkie* by William Burroughs, *Confessions of an Opium Eater* by De Quincy and *On the Road* by Jack Kerouac.

All great art has common qualities of authenticity, honesty and truth. The banal, counterfeit and fake, are the stuff of sentimentality, and thereby render themselves ultimately as the crocodile tears of artistic merit and worth.

Ultimately a writer's best friend is the good quality work that he is engaged in at any given time. This gives him a sense of self-esteem and self-respect, and acts as a raft which helps him to keep afloat when the seas of life are stormy.

When Knut Hamsun was writing his classic, *Hunger*, and undergoing hallucinations from food deprivation, he still possessed in his consciousness an artistic worth which motivated him to continue.

In the case of Jean Genet and *The Thief's Journal*, written in various jails under gruelling sub-human prison conditions, the author possessed an in-built sense of worth and belief in the dog-eared and excrement-smeared manuscripts. When they were confiscated and destroyed by the prison guards he had to commence again from the beginning.

Writers must contend with the problems of loneliness,

discouragement, disappointment and failure. As some wise critic has pointed out, the only writers worth encouraging are those who will not give up.

It is frequently said by writers and literary aficionados that if writing was easy, then it would invite many more practitioners. The fact remains it is not, not only in its execution but also in its design, concept and architecture.

This country of ours has been particularly blessed in its crop of major and gifted scribes. It is often questioned as to why this is so: the allied innuendo is that maybe we are overly rich in talented wordsmiths.

If the situation was reversed and our national literary reservoir was dry, seeking disciples to whet its appetite, then one of the major thrusts of the enquiry would be why do we not have any great writers, and even if we do why are they all dead?

If the departed could speak from the regions of the after-life, or the confines of their current abode, perhaps they would be narrating how the story was really not a story at all, but part of a deeper pathological compulsion to bend the perimeters of consciousness like Joyce into a creation of the imagination which has much to do with our inherent genius as a people, as it does with any one writer's style or books.

Certainly most great works of literature were arrived at through their technique and shape by a circuitous route. The journey was perhaps a pilgrimage, a tribute to a solitary trail into the hinterland of the soul.

The canopy of all art is life, what happens in the tent of the artist's creation is his own affair. But writers provide with their camels the means for the world to cross its deserts.

ART, BOHEMIANS AND ARTISTS

ALBERT CAMUS in one of his short stories, describes at its beginning a writer writing a short story, somewhat a novel idea. The opening line goes with a literary dilemma for the dubious author, "Did the horse prance or did the horse dance?"

The writer did not proceed beyond this stage of verbiage, but Camus's story proceeded admirably to a full and rounded ending. To achieve with writing takes more than a pen and a blank sheet of paper, or indeed the most stream-lined modern computer.

Sometimes I think art and writing is a bit like being a weight-lifter of modest but significant stature. The success of the enterprise depends greatly on ideas, to refer again to Camus in his book *The Rebel*: "strength comes from ideas."

Like the struggling weight-lifter confronted by the task on hand, every time you try it there is the possibility of failure. Even as you attempt the lift, one muscle wilting, one thought-process lost, may lead ingloriously to a missed opportunity. And even if the artistic dumb-bells are raised above your head in an Olympic triumph, who really cares? The point is, you do, that's why you put in all that effort.

Little did Emily Dickinson or Franz Kafka know while they lived that posthumously their work would illumine the literary world. They both published almost nothing while alive. The moral, if there is one: a seed of artistic worth when planted may not take hold until much later.

Nevertheless, what Tolstoy said about religion is also true of art – "Religion comes from life, not life from religion." To refer again to Kafka – "I have got many books from life, but very little life from books."

William Butler Yeats said that, "When a poet remakes a line of poetry, he is remaking himself." Art infers an immediate form of creativity in whatever discipline is invoked. But also implicit in its structure is a self-improvement on the part of the true artist.

Sometimes perhaps the art form is a link in a chain of realised peak experiences. Not exclusive to only artists, but the creative highs and lows shared by those who lead very unexpressed lives that never surface in any form of art.

They trudge through the tedium, boredom and frustration of their daily round with the relief of humour and romance, added to a network of enmity, friendship, loyalty and family unity and feuding often leading to disunity. Through their collective hidden agendas they create a receptacle for the stuff of art, and the diet which the artist has created on his or her menu.

As with some painters like the French impressionists or poets and writers like Paul Valéry and Baudelaire, Dylan Thomas, Brendan Behan and Paddy Kavanagh could be added to the roll of honour of low-heeled aristocracy who left a valuable legacy to the world.

This distinguished academy would probably be amiable to songwriters, like Shane MacGowan, Kris Kristofferson, Neil Young, Leonard Cohen, Bob Dylan and Phil Lynott. A New Orleans jazz veteran like Louis Armstrong, Duke Ellington, Charlie Parker, lyricist Cole Porter, a blues titan like BB

King or blues guitarists like Leadbelly or Mississippi John Hurt, or poets like Ferlinghetti, Corso, Kerouac, Snyder and Ginsberg.

If Shane MacGowan had taken the pledge and promised, like the Irish navvy, inveterate drinker in Camden Town, at the bequest of a toffee-nosed magistrate "not even to have the teenchiest weenchiest drop of sherry before dinner," he probably could not have written one of the greatest songs of this era, "Fairytale of New York." It is set in a drunk tank, with the rejects of humanity oozing the pus of pain and failure from their pores and their life shattered experiences exchanged in brain-damaged smiles, dislocated drunken speech and stories of twisted dreams and pulverised lies of misery and pain. It crystallises, through a personal addiction of self with insight into the agony of others, into a beautiful song. Incorporating humanity and courage, this takes a great talent which is unique and will live forever in people's hearts.

Similarly, if Kris Kristofferson did not know the all-encompassing descending dark cloud of a mind fogged by drink and feelings of guilt, remorse, loss and regret, he could not have written a song for the world to hear like "Sunday Morning Coming Down." Perhaps as anyone who has been close to death – spiritual or physical – knows it injects a desperate appetite for rebirth, incorporated into a kind of preventative form of suicide. The latter is often what happens with the birth of an embryo of a great artistic creation.

Mozart's "Requiem" was written on his death bed. Padraig Pearse wrote one of his best poems, "The Mother," awaiting execution in Kilmainham Gaol. More recently, the Nigerian poet and playwright, Ken Sarawiwa, wrote some of his best poems just before he was ignobly hanged.

Artists sometimes cursed by poverty, adverse and tragic circumstances, have changed through courage and belief in what is worthy and just. The course of other lives similarly affected in a way that makes living a bit more tolerable and happy for a lot of people.

SO YOU'D LIKE TO BE A POET

GEORGE BERNARD SHAW was once approached by an aspiring poet after a lecture. The man gave Shaw a sheaf of poems. "Would you say I am a poet, Mr Shaw?" enquired the novice hopefully.

"How old are you?" asked the literary giant.

When the young man replied nineteen, Shaw quipped, "Well, you know a lot of young people write poetry when they are nineteen or twenty, but if you are still writing poetry when you are forty then maybe you are a poet."

Poetry and its midwife the muse very often have a difficult birth; which is also true of poets. According to Rilke "If somebody wants to be a poet, he should lie in his bed at night, look into his heart and say to himself, that he shall be nothing else except a poet." Miscarriages are frequent, with the toll of life's obstacles on the fledgling verse makers.

Some similarities however, seem to be common to the species. If one of the pre-requisites of a good dentist, carpenter or surgeon is a steady hand, it is desirable that a good poet should have a loving heart accompanied by a somewhat commendable set of sensibilities to regulate and appropriate his or her emotions.

My experience has often included unsociable hours, working conditions which no union would tolerate and an income which is certainly not in line with the minimum wage of any developed country.

Sometimes the more stressful an experience the greater its ease into poetic form. Poets also have a right to food, shelter and a little money. It is impossible to write well if one is constantly fretting and harassed by the basic needs of survival. Surely Arts Councils, patrons of the arts and also governments exist for this reason.

According to Ho Chi Minh: "It is not enough for a poet to write a poem, he must also be able to lead an attack." That attack it could also be said might be on the poet's own legion of bad adjectives, or army of weak images.

If, as most schoolboys know, Wordsworth's dictum is true: "Poetry is emotion recollected in tranquillity," then poetry is the turbulent upheaval fashioned in the furnace of passion, and the smithy of the subconscious. Federico Garcia Lorca, the revolutionary Spanish poet, said: "If prose is reality, then poetry is truth." While another school of thought says: "If prose is communication then poetry is communion."

The mystery of "what is poetry?" haunts poets and scholars alike. As GK Chesterton says in his essay on bad poetry and verse: "It is much easier to arrive at a lucid awareness of what is weak and shoddy in the art than to come to a full appreciation of what is good." It becomes dangerous if not fatal to question too much its mysterious source. It is a river, certainly, which begins in some mountain-top of the heart and soul, sometimes wedged between the granite of angst and the metal of torture, then becomes a trickle of inspiration. But there is no definitive answer to the question.

If indeed there was a supermarket for the emotions, poetry and all art would become a dispensable utility overnight, just like toothpaste, after-shave lotion, washing-up liquid or toilet rolls. Happily this is not so and as long as there is the mystery of man, with his monumental struggle to survive, there will continue to be poets.

What is the roughage of the human condition for many people – unhappy love, death and all the array of misfortune – is often the inspiration of poetry. But it is by his work that the would-be poet shall ultimately be judged by carping critics and loyal supporters alike. "Irish poets learn your trade/Sing whatever is well made," says Yeats.

If the successful poet is the one who remains most loyal to his truest feelings, at their deepest levels, then the failure of the illustrious tribe is the one who betrays his emotions either in literature or life or both, for thirty pieces of silver.

In company with a worthy set of sensibilities referred to earlier, a calm disposition is required in order to make it possible to sustain an idea from its inception to the moment of poetic verse.

As in any other area of human activity problems proliferate, like flies around cow-dung at the height of summer, jealousy, politicking, black hatreds, careerism, and backstabbing, these are all part of the poet's burden. The confraternity of letters is certainly not a happy family united in its strength. Much more like a divided and squabbling clan with its own factions and family feuding.

It nevertheless has its compensations in small luxuries: the "job satisfaction," or when one of the literary embryos is successful, or perhaps when a reading strikes a deeply responsive chord or indeed even an essay such as this.

The trick, insofar as there is one, is to be aware of a sense of self-discipline – with a very long leash; wielding control on occasions with a very tight rein, or at other junctures allowing the muse a free rein. But always clinging, however feebly, to the reins, so as to prevent the beast from running into the sunset and oblivion.

For all the pangs of anxiety which the insecurities of such a precarious way of life bring with it, there is also below the innocuous seeming lethargic surface, teeming subterranean activity at work, some Vesuvius waiting to erupt onto the blank page.

But above all it is vital to participate in the human race, that is by its very nature creative rather than destructive, unlike the festering sores of moneyed corruption that plague the world. Poets may not be Yuppies, but then the good Lord, himself quite a poet, never intended them to be.

THE STRUGGLE FOR
THE LEGAL TENDER

"NEITHER a borrower nor a lender be."

So goes the famous quote of Polonius in *Hamlet*, his advice to his son Laertes, setting out on his journey to France. Polonius was nicely cushioned from the harsh realities of economics as the head honcho in the house of Elsinore. Such advice was easy for him to give.

Daily people do borrow, from each other, credit unions, banks, building societies and other unconventional sources, as and when severe need demands. On occasions they cannot pay back, and enter into the slippery descent of the debtor's swamp.

One American president opined: "The business of government is business; if true, then the ordinary citizen cannot be condemned for trying to make ends meet as best he can, even if the enterprise is fraught with risk and peril."

Among the stories about Brendan Behan which abound in Dublin is the one about him not having the largesse to pay the taxi driver. He simply left his typewriter in the boot in lieu of the debt and redeemed it the following day.

Although pawn shops do not proliferate as freely as they once did, they still exist. They also engage in a lively retail trade collected from items which are never salvaged, so helping the creation of the annual profits.

"Give unto Caesar what is Caesar's," but sometimes it

seems Caesar has just a little bit more than he needs, and a lot of deserving people do not. The fashionable philosophy of Yuppyism seems to be the shark with the biggest bite rules the seas.

As the gap between the rich and the poor increases, it follows that the marginalised and disenfranchised become more desperate. Theirs is a concealed world and often unexpressed agenda of need and impaired human dignity. They are the piglets that James Joyce talked about when writing about Ireland, "the sow that eats her farrow."

Indeed, the black economy for a lot of people is very often not dark at all, but provides the only crock of gold complete with rainbow that they are likely to get. It is well known that the dispossessed do not have a voice, as political power is synonymous with economic power, so they are out of the frame. Like Orwell's *Animal Farm*, "we are all equal but some animals are more equal than others."

Disadvantaged neighbourhoods usually end up getting bad press. Invariably they have no press of their own – so they are forbidden to testify to their own authenticity. They are like a person trying to contact a busy switchboard: if they leave a message its import and sensitivity is thwarted, garbled and usually distorted.

Marshal McLuhan, the intellectual doyen and prophet of the Sixties, in his book *The Medium Is the Message*, wrote that television is a hot medium. If this is true, then it has a vested interest in boiling news. Radio, on the other hand, is a cool medium, and arguably a very good friend to many people.

Merely because beleaguered members of God's little flock of homo sapiens respond to bureaucracy and red tape with a sharp scissors of ingenuity and panache, it does not mean that they are less honest than a white collar worker who pays his or her tax on a regular basis. Perhaps it might mean in reality if life's little quirks had placed them as a senior person in a semi-State body, they might make a more honest and full tax return.

Father McDyer in Glen Colmcille in County Donegal successfully harnessed native energy, into a co-operative workers' organisation with the main concern that people should have employment with reasonable reward and working conditions. Who can say that the work force was meant to work sun up to sun down for little or no reward?

It might be true that material poverty belies an intellectual poverty of ideas, which could inspire and enthuse an improvement in many a bleak economic situation. If the general outline of our economic blueprint is a state that has very sharp claws, like a bird of prey more interested in the hunt, rather than honouring all the participants who must be cherished through the age-old practice.

There is a school of thought that holds the opinion that the only place socialism works is in a beehive or an ant-hill. Now it seems with all the economic pesticides of conservatism, the very existence of these havens of natural sanctuary are under threat.

Within the fabric of pure Communism as obtained in a monastic setting, or indeed Buddhist or neo-Christian, there are no custodial penalties of imprisonment or capital punishment. The dignity and moral rights of the members are acknowledged under a strict religious and moral code. It is not the philosophy of an eye for an eye or a tooth for a tooth. Rather if somebody wants to borrow, let him or her borrow. Let he who has two coats give unto him who has none.

In the Christian annals of gospel truths there are seven deadly sins — they have intruded from time immemorial on the harmonious relations and happiness of people, to the point of holding people's welfare at gun point and under threat of violence and murder.

If society as we know it is dangling dangerously on a precipice of imminent disaster albeit the Peace Process, drugs, crime, robbery of old people, cowardly materialism, greed and selfishness, then the second millennium augurs strange forebodings for the planet.

Birds will still sing cheerfully on summer mornings, rabbits will leap and run with joy on hillsides, children will play happily.

They, like people, will be trying to forage and provide for the young as best they can. Some creature, human or otherwise, will be under threat, and ultimately all these things pass. One thing it is not possible to borrow, is time, when it has rushed past you in such a hurry that renders borrowing, out of the question.

IS THERE LIFE AFTER DEBT?

STONE AGE MAN bartered and engaged in his daily business using stones, with a hole cut in the centre. Fred and Wilma Flintstone of their day must have had very real and major problems to cope with.

Whether it was the rising price of dinosaur meat or the huge increase in the costs of turtles eggs, also perhaps included was how to get the kids a cave of their own close to a river and a forest with plenty of wood so they could light a fire and keep themselves warm on cold winter nights.

There must have been passionate and fiery arguments in the cave late at night. About why sometimes the elusive stones with the much sought after hole were not rolling in — is that where the expression "stony broke" originates.

As a new millennium dawns, the economics of the world have not changed greatly for many Wilmas and Freds, or indeed Seans and Maureens, still trying desperately to make ends meet in a financial equation that defies logic.

It is part of folklore that he who pays the piper calls the tune, presumably this also means that if the piper is out of tune he does not get paid. So it becomes obvious the most popular tune is money. But be consoled, some of the best tunes were written by people who were not gifted with the Midas touch. To their everlasting credit, they left something much more valuable than their debts behind them.

If Mozart had been Oasis in high society Vienna, he might

not have made out. But if Mozart had been Oasis today, he would be coining a fair penny, to recompense him for times of financial duress and a lean diet.

When the little financial alarm bells start hammering, gently at first, then the crescendo builds up gradually, to a deafening climax. "Life Without the Doh, Rey, Me," the title of a song in which Woody Guthrie wrote about the all-powerful dollar bill. The song written about the depression in the Thirties is about American and migrant workers in Oklahoma being checked at the Californian border for collateral. As we all know, today more than ever, a lack of fiscal rectitude can open like a concealed trap-door in your soul through which not only you but many a good man can disappear.

This neighbourhood I live in, in Dublin's south inner city, is rampant with problems, unemployment, crime, housing, drugs, but there is the aspect of the miraculous on a daily basis; a kind of courageous refusal to give up even if the Sheriff or the bailiff are at the door. Some simple valuable things cannot be confiscated or taken away, a smile, a sense of humour, a kind word – knowing when to turn off to the world and its ways and chill out and relax in whatever you construe as a safety valve, that does not blow your mind completely.

Fred and Wilma Flintstone must have had damn good nights in their cave with whatever substances that passed their lips and made them happy. The words of Abraham Lincoln "most folks are as happy as they want to be." Maybe one thing that your creditors do not want you to be is happy or even if they do, it's at a price you cannot afford. But if you don't want to be happy yourself then it's time to drop in on the local Sheriff and give yourself up voluntarily.

In the segregated New Orleans parish prison, one of the toughest in America, I got a free education, the likes of which is not available in any major Ivy League university.

Many a struggling student gets into debt while in college, so rendering studying impossible. Perhaps as astute and innovative course for young freshman students in today's world might be, how to avoid getting into debt, or once in debt, how to get out of it.

"The shark has such pearly teeth dear and keeps them pearly white". So goes Satchmo's great song. Just like the shark in Louis's song, money lenders and banks keep their teeth out of sight until they are ready to bite you.

Cardinal Wolseley, in the film *A Man for All Seasons,* written by Robert Bolt starred Orson Wells and Paul Schofield as Thomas More. When Thomas asked Cardinal Wolsey, played by Orson Wells, how he would close down the monasteries in Henry VIII's England, the reply was simply one word – "Pressure."

So debt just like a kind of material closure of the cloisters of freedom, incorporates at its worst, the pressure of being unfree. In a world where freedom is a dwindling commodity for many people.

But perhaps when the door of material freedom closes, then there is still a cloud with a silver lining available, so many people hope. *Spec est vitae ancora*, hope is the anchor of life.

Is there life after debt, there has to be proved by negation and deprivation of life during debt. A story recorded in the Liberties here in Dublin, an area full of colourful stories tells of a visitor to a fuel merchants in the locality enquiring after seeing the somewhat defeated aspect to the personalities visiting the premises. He asked, "What keeps these people going, they all seem to have no money and want turf?"

The experienced businessman shrewdly replied, "It's not getting the turf, it's trying to get it that keeps them going."

CITY LIFE – BITTERSWEET

WILSHIRE BOULEVARD in Los Angeles can be a hauntingly desolate and lonely place, or indeed 5th Avenue in New York City, Yonge Street in Toronto or Market Street in San Francisco, and the main streets in our own native metropolis of Dublin.

Leeson Street, Grafton Street or O'Connell Street in their solitary refrain of human footsteps act as a quiet orchestration of the human heart. The ultimate quality of any city is its indigenous population with their own desperation and their own struggles.

Dublin is a great city as portrayed in literature from Joyce to O'Casey to Behan. But it is only Dubliners who can really get under the skin of the anatomy of bittersweet life: the innocence, guilt, poverty, tragedy, heartbreak and love which is modern Dublin.

The most modest perception of city life shows that respectability in its real sense, or indeed virtue and morality, these attributes are not essentially packaged in Christian Dior cocktail dresses or Louis Copeland suits.

More likely it is as true, in Dublin as elsewhere, that the server is more gifted and talented than the customer who is being served. This is the result of the mischievous artful deception of city life with its primary concerns for efficiency and a veneer of organisation and not a little greed.

Surely a true definition of culture attempts to embroider

the human sensibilities with a decorative and tasteful cloak of honesty and truth, for people to exhibit and enjoy. But the nature of the exercise if it is to be successful, requires attention to the details of human existence.

As a nation we claim to enshrine the tenets of Christianity and democracy in our constitution. But what is Christian or democratic about the plight of emigration, unemployment or the molestation of children which abounds in our society?

Every day in Dublin life is seen through differing tinted lenses as experiences vary for its citizens. Problems for many are monumental, hugely impossible and insoluble.

A child with a cardboard box begging on O'Connell Bridge begins the day searching for the means of survival on a cold winter's morning. Then in the evening must return to an alcoholic home to be greeted by the twin siblings of violence and alcoholism.

In comfortable three-star hotel lounges in Dublin 2 and 4, the bourgeoisie relax with a mixture of affluence, self-indulgence and discontent. The slender balance of an undefined spirituality that is as elusive as the Yeti in the Himalayas seems to escape the appetite of the rich and the poor in this city.

If money and power are the aphrodisiacs of the financial barons who function, manipulate and control in boardrooms and from behind mahogany desks, then a modicum of modest clothing of self-respect and dignity is what the poor seek.

The bars in this city possess a world-wide and universal condition of halting and hesitatingly imperfect emotions which needs perfection of love as suitable companions and friends.

As a signature of our individual autograph of distinction, we laugh, hate, mock and ridicule. Yet it remains that we are great, simply because so many care and try to live out lives that are heroic because they are difficult and painful and still possess a sense of humour.

Dublin can be observed and understood clearly at one's leisure on a pleasant summer's afternoon in St Stephen's Green in the heart of the city. It is rather like a wondrous and hugely rich fruit cake. The ingredients are a great variety of human additions, cherries, raisins, sultanas and a little alcohol, but like any self-respecting fruit cake of quality an indispensable component is a generous helping of nuts!

As people walk trepiditiously towards a new century with undefined mysteries in our history and character, our destination is unclear. We are attributed with an unlimited friendliness towards tourists and visitors from abroad, with the occasional or indeed frequent mugging, handbag snatching, car theft and even the crime of murder thrown in.

It is feasible that our friendliness and veneer of amiability is really an escape valve to prevent us from dwelling on the darker sides of our own personality; a psychological decoy of temperament in-built into a kind of character that is a little rudderless, because it has been misled and misguided.

On this beautiful late May Sunday afternoon, as I look around St Stephen's Green, the children are happy, playing, so full of promise for the future. The old have lived their lives laced with regret and angst. Families in small groups consolidate their strengths with a high degree of levity and humour. Even if we never get it all right we can know that we have a little bit of it right.

WE ALL NEED OUR OWN SPACE

"IF PEOPLE only knew of the spaceless heaven under their noses," thus wrote the poet Patrick Kavanagh. Conversely then, people would be spared some of their involuntary descent into the vast overcrowding of some of their hellish experiences.

The words of Desiderata, "Go placidly amid the noise and haste – and remember what peace there is in solitude." We all know, presumably, that being Buddha on a mountain top is not accessible to most people, but if you act as Buddha on a busy city street then you really are Buddha.

A frequent modern vocal plea from some unfortunate stressed, stifled person under unmanageable duress is, "I need my own space." We all know the symptoms, the pressure between the shoulder blades that achingly becomes a headache, resulting in a throb in the temple, and the beleaguered person feels they should be on draught Valium or side orders of Ecstasy tablets.

When the barometer of anxiety rises so high it is in danger of breaking the glass, like trapped rats we human beings can display some very ignoble traits indeed. We might feel like strangling a bawling child, or bumping off a slow-moving pensioner in a fast-moving world, when we are trying under pressure to make the checkout counter in a hurry in the supermarket.

The main reason people are short-changed of their rightful share of space is other people. Very often competing for the same space, whether it be economic, occupational, social, aesthetic, spiritual or cultural. Patrick Street in Cork or O'Connell

Street in Dublin at the height of the rush hour might seem to be a kind of apocalyptic augury of the demise of mankind.

So many urgent, almost homicidal tendencies to preserve a unique life force – all in a fight to the death in competition with each other. The context of savage battle is only exacerbated in Oxford Street in London or Fifth Avenue, New York or indeed, the subways of Tokyo at peak rush hour.

Buddha spent a long time under the Bodhi tree before enlightenment. But the meditations he initiated were to prove a lot more beneficial for humanity than gold dust in a miser's pocket. Similarly, the lines from Leonard Cohen, "Jesus was a sailor and he spent a long time watching, from his lonely wooden tower."

Women and men, the alleged princesses and princes of the world – tend to be territorial creatures. There is conflict when spaces are intruded upon and privacy is violated, especially when there is property involved. Resultant discord, anger, argument, aggression, violence – domestic, institutional, criminal, mostly territorial ultimately culminating in war.

The cat and the mouse have their own space which interchanges and is a variable juxtaposition of feline and rodent modus operandi and behaviour. The success of Tom and Gerry cartoons is their endless effervescent ability to entertain – perhaps partly because it sublimates into laughter the torture and hurt we inflict on each other.

Sport often for its gladiatorial combatants depends for its most vital moments on a use of space. Sometimes the most crucial victory deciding dramatic moments, depend just how creatively and ingeniously a very limited space is used.

In his book about bullfighting in Spain, *Death in the Afternoon*, Hemingway explains, "The bull has his terrain and the matador also possesses his own terrain. As long as the bull does not invade the matador's terrain and the matador does not invade the bull's terrain then there is no problem."

But, some people are a little like over-confident matadors, they deliberately wave red rags at quiet and placid inoffensive types of people. Little do they know it, but there is a potential bull in everybody who is capable of goring the opposition. "The West shall shake the East awake/While ye have the night for morn." These are James Joyce's words about China – a country that knows a lot about overcrowding.

Mental space as well as spiritual is vital for us all. Unlike our forebears, nowadays noise pollution is something that encroaches on our little citadel of serenity. Pneumatic drills or ambulance sirens do not chime as the tubular bells bade the people to come to prayer in a Tibetan monastery in Lhasa.

I can recall standing overlooking a free-for-all freeway network in Los Angeles early in the morning, like a forerunner of Spaghetti Junction. Where is everybody going in such a hurry, I thought, and anyway what are they going to do when they get there? The truth is I still don't know – and I honestly don't think anybody else does either.

Jack Kerouac, author of *On the Road*, once said, "the duty of youth is to explore." Presumably by this he also meant new vistas and frontiers of undiscovered space of intellect, art, and new pastures of peace and happiness.

Perhaps in a way, life is like a series of windows we observe through. Each view is different yet similar and connected to the space of heaven that Patrick Kavanagh referred to at the beginning of this article. For everybody at some time, the glass shatters, for some more than others. But there is a bit of heaven as well as hell available, it depends on us – and the way we see.

THE WINNERS TELL THE JOKES; THE LOSERS MAKE THEIR OWN ARRANGEMENTS

SOME PEOPLE go through life without indulging in a light-hearted flutter on a horse, a dog or a game of poker. Perhaps the exception is the Grand National or another notable turf event, the Derby.

From my early teens, a tanner as a small wager on a horse in the bookie's office at the bottom of our street was an acceptable social outlet. Lester Piggot often obliged, as did Doug Smith, since gone from the racing scene.

Psychologists are of the opinion that a little wager is a good thing, some kind of release from the stresses and strains of living. Obviously they do not recommend addiction. It seems to be the case that some personalities are more prone to problem gambling than others, even if the subject of the addict's choice had to be invented. Yet it is a timeless human involvement. How are we to know that pre-historic man did not engage in turtle racing at short odds!

People, mostly the male variety of the Irish species, turn to the precarious wheel of the gambling classes for different reasons. There is on record the category of gambler in the form of the bored housewife or lonely spinster or bachelor who frequent amusement parlours and the silent rows of one-armed bandits for recourse to thrill-seeking.

In Dublin and other cities there is the facility of morning

and afternoon Bingo, removed from the evening "social" session in the local parish hall. The housekeeping money can be washed away in a deluge of pitiful artificial substitutions for the more real ingredients of living and happiness.

The rich and super-rich frequent casinos with roulette, blackjack and other enticements of pleasure and frivolity that relieve the wealthy of their assets.

From Gibraltar to Aberdeen, from Reno to Vegas there is a constant stream of adorers who come to worship at the altar of the Goddess, Lady Luck. Between the placing of the wager and betting chips and the wheel's last click, there is the atlas of the world's emotions on display.

The appetite to gamble is endemic to human nature – it is not confined to any one class. Sport in all its facets is a fair target of the gambling classes and a major focus of the punter's interest.

The classic characterisation of the bookie with his open leather bag stuffed with notes – tenners and twenties – wearing a Crombie overcoat, moustache, and a red rose in his buttonhole, is emulated only by the parish priest and a handful of like-minded clerics from seminary days indulging in a social outing at the racecourse away from the daily grind of chores.

Amongst the Orientals, especially the Chinese who have settled in this country, is a voracious appetite for gambling. They populate the betting outlets in Dublin heavily, like bygone disciples of Buddha or Confucius. Nowadays they are part of the Godhead of Paddy Power, Terry Rogers, Ladbrokes and Baggot Racing.

Neither are pool and snooker exempt from their diet. They include sizeable wagers on the multi-coloured spheres which they guide with their skill. I have heard a story about the fate of two Chinese takeaways being decided on a black ball game.

For myself, one landmark was risking my last tenner – after a couple of losses – on Willie Shoemaker, in an attempt to buy my Matric for my Mature University Arts course. Willie turned up trumps and seemed to re-cross every horse in the race with his genius. So he got a beautiful, clear, victorious ride to the line.

For a writer and indeed any student of our species, the ordinary betting office offers myriad opportunities for study. The eyes are a clue in their desperation and hope, the pained grimace of the face muscles as a horse falls or becomes outpaced. But then there is the feeling of a smile pinned to the heart, with the sweet success of a winner.

ON THE SET

"QUIET!" The shrill voice fills the reverential poignant scene in Lincoln Prison, 1919, with actors, Aidan Grenell as the priest and Alan Rickman as the young Eamon de Valera. The voice on the wings of the scene, once again, this time more shrill and strident, was raised a decibel higher. "QUIET PLEASE!" A male voice, serious but more controlled and authoritative, not so shrill, quotes the scene number. Before this there is the shrill voice once again. "Cameras Rolling!" Neil Jordan's voice from his director's vantage, watching the scene on a monitor, issues the supreme command of a Caesar – ACTION!

The priest intones the Eucharist mantra in Latin. Their verbiage is full of humanity, dignity and very moving. Alan Rickman rings the communion bell, I am one of the nine Republican prisoners on bended knees. I dutifully and reverentially bow my head on the cue of the bell. My knees are rapidly losing the argument with the hard granite floor. My head is still bowed, the cue was clear. But now I ask myself what is the cue to resurface. The cue is unclear. I make a one-eyed reconnaissance around at the other heads which are raised. So, sheep-like, I follow suit.

The scene continues to the wine transubstantiation with more bowing of heads and the bell rings again. The scene comes to an end. Neil Jordan's voice fills the small, narrow corridor in Kilmainham Jail with its eerie, authentic and oppressive sense of confinement. The director is not happy.

He gently chides his clutch of extras for the day, drawn from mixed and varied backgrounds. Jack, to my left in prison uniform made from American army blankets, is a playwright. He has radio success behind him, but not as yet the Abbey Theatre. John nearby is from Ballymun. He is also interested in play-writing. The lean, bearded intellectual adjacent is a young engineer working in Frankfurt. He is home on holiday but dislikes Frankfurt.

The director explains. "Some of you are not bowing your heads when you are supposed to." He continues, "When the host is raised, then you bow your heads." This is true also for the wine. His displeasure is only mild. He is not a Captain Ahab and seems quietly satisfied that the ingredients are in the bowl for a take on the next shot.

On a point of order, his instructions contradict those of Pat, the assistant director, who directed that the heads should be bowed on the cue of the bell.

This film has a twenty-five-million-pound budget like *Michael Collins*, currently being shot in and around Dublin, starring superstars like Julia Roberts and Liam Neeson and with major international investment, and also directed by Neil Jordan. By contrast, a low-budget film like *Poitín*, a minor classic of a genre, produced by Bob Quinn and starring Niall Tóibín, Donal McCann and the late and much-lamented Cyril Cusack.

These productions, although vastly different in theme and dramatic thrust, depend heavily on the goodwill and generosity of low-heeled, marginalised talent — extras. Although undiscovered they have been badly bitten by the artistic bite, so are consequently very willing serfs for major international money lords. Even to less well-heeled but talented directors and producers desperately trying to generate filthy lucre.

Compare the dying wish of an alcoholic for the price of a drink in the early morning house on the quays to the simple grub-steak entrance fee into the hall of fame where egos are nurtured and fattened among podgy levels of comfort, if not decadence, with cocaine, champagne and orange juice, villas, Jacuzzis, yachts and sex and more sex.

The film business has now become a multi-million pound industry in Ireland. And just like all other capitalistic entrepreneurial exercises, it will always have winners and losers and victims. A director or producer, just like a jockey on the favourite in a horse race quite often has to be very ruthless for his mount to be first past the post. Especially if there is a photo finish in the form of a serious, if not chronic, budgeting shortfall.

Art has its own twilight zone of failure, heartbreak and disappointment. The subtle grey areas are very often unexpressed, more perhaps than any other profession or career. Consider the *Big Issues* seller on a busy street in Dublin, Cork or London. He or she may be feeling their guts churn with fear, anxiety and stress about the prospect of spending yet another night in a Simon shelter or a homeless hostel or a friend's floor if they cannot come up with the back rent, yet he or she must appear cheerful. Similarly, the extra waiting patiently in a queue in the Actors' Equity office in Liberty Hall, Dublin may be quietly blowing a very gifted mind, fretting that the movie world may never be afforded the grace and benefit of their talents. It is a poor consolation to think *Anyway who cares in a busy, indifferent, psychopathic and greedy world?*

The wardrobe ladies have been busy all morning with meticulous attention to detail, as have the hairdressers. On the set, the director and the assistant are making adjustments of the kneeling prisoners, from one knee chalk mark on the concrete floor to another.

It is not generally known that the diet of the prisoners who were incarcerated in Kilmainham Jail, like the 1916 leaders, was a cold diet. In the famine years, nine thousand inmates died in this place which is now a national monument. If there was to be an escape, it had to be in the first six months of captivity, otherwise the strength to scale the walls would have ebbed too much to have made the effort.

On arrival in the morning at 6.00am, breakfast was provided in portable sandwich-style containers, but had to be abandoned along the way. Mobile phones were as evident, as pieces of confetti at a wedding. The transparency and hollowness of film people at any time can be a little offensive, rather like the discomfort of a sensitive novice nun in a harem.

My sojourn into the world of the housewife or an unmarried mother or a person on the dole working as an extra has been fortunate in one way. One group of extras working on this film got so fed up after waiting around for ten interminable hours that they voluntarily severed their contract and just split. The tedium got the upper hand and they got out, presumably without pay.

I am left to marvel at how major films are made – the dedication, hard work and commitment of so many talented professional people. Art is hard work. The end product needs an audience. But only the very gifted and marginally insane are possessed with the dynamics of personality to bring a project like this to fruition. You can see it in your living room or local cinema. Even then it is you who are the jury of opinion about its worth – the audience.

THE SUMMER OF 1969

THE FULL and crowded memories, like a bell ringing noisily on a cable car, jangling as it goes up, then down: the severe incline of hills on the sunny busy streets of San Francisco. In the cable-car's cramped space, hanging on for dear life as tightly as possible to the hand-holder close to the roof. In case you might lose this part of your valued space in this beautiful city. A world with exotic delights and all the excitement of adventure with its hidden secrets, heartbreak and cracked dreams.

I was earning a living as a bus boy with tips in a restaurant adjacent to Union Square: always new and a glittering experience. Burt Lancaster, tanned, with film star grooming, walked past me into the restaurant on the graveyard shift that I was working. The Grateful Dead and Jerry Garcia playing the Filmore West on the same bill as Miles Davis, again in Marin County. Miles with his trumpet celebrating with soul music the Easter Sunday morning resurrection.

The Palace of the Legion of Honour took my breath away. I saw for the first time Rodin's *Thinker* and *Gazelles*. The idyllic moments of youth high on the top of Mount Tamalpias in Marin County, viewing the spectacle and majesty of the setting sun sliding into oblivion on the Pacific Ocean. San Francisco Bay, ships setting out and coming home under the Golden Gate Bridge, with access to the vast Pacific Ocean and all parts of the world. The subdued and understated terror of San Quentin Prison, a clean-coloured den of no freedom visible way down below from the summit of the mountain-top in sunny twilight. In Golden Gate Park watching the cast of *Hair* putting all their considerable talents to maximum power in songs like "The Age of Aquarius."

The Native American Indians staged a protest and took over Alcatraz Prison. The Dubliners visited and played for the real citizens of America on the Rock. Afterwards Ronnie Drew, John Sheahan, Barney McKenna and Co visited the general hang-out in Sausalito, the Trident Restaurant. John Sheahan enquired, "what's the soup like?" with his doleful look. Later at a shindig high in the hills of Marin County I met Black Elk and Thunder Hawk. The latter had an exquisite charm and good looks all his own which later served him well in a movie career. Ronnie Drew, with his effervescent bubbling personality, loquaciously articulated to a spellbound group how he could talk to the horses he had at home in Ireland. Luke Kelly waxed lyrical to a captivated audience about the marvellous feelings he was feeling, to the merriment and fascination of the assembled party-goers. Around dawn, with a general sense of fatigue and exhaustion, the party ended in a taxi travelling towards San Francisco. Jake, the black taxi-driver, broke the news gently to Ronnie how much the tab would be. The bearded minstrel was aghast. It was a great night, one of the very many in the summer of 1969.

In support of the Indians' demands for civil liberties in Clyde Memorial Church in downtown San Francisco, a major poetry reading took place. It included Lawrence Ferlinghetti, accompanied by an auto harp, rendering a poem titled "Big Sur Sunset Trip." At intervals the poem reached a crescendo by the chanting of the Holy Hindu Mantra *OM*, giving the live music and voice a n almost Godlike power. The Pulitzer Prize-winning poet, Gary Synder read poems in native American dialect and language with considerable skill. The poet Gregory Corso rendered his eulogy to

Jack Kerouac who had recently died, which included the line "Jack, nothing happened in America which you did not know."

The Japanese Tea Gardens with the charm of the Japanese tea-servers dressed in bright floral-pattemed kimonos. The fortune cookies that contained a paper inscription with some possible insight into the mystery of a young man's life. The long hesitant twilights of Sausalito that lingered almost forever and left seemingly involuntarily. A poster pinned on the wall in the San Francisco Arts Institute seemed to sum up much of the swell of romance and dreams. It was a poem by Gary Synder titled "Smoky the Bear Sutra" with the line, "Be kind to animals, children, and prisoners."

In front of City Hall in downtown San Francisco a political protest took place close to the Financial District. Country Joe McDonald (without the Fish, as they were resting) included songs like "What Are We Fighting For? I Don't Give a Damn, Next Stop Is Vietnam."

The well-known student leader Tom Hayden, President of Students for a Democratic Society, addressed the audience, where he told the assembly, "whatever happens now is just Laurel and Hardy stuff." Later on he became an elected representative in the Californian State Legislature. Present also with musical accompaniment was Allen Ginsburg, bearded and guru-like, happily singing the lines "Merrily, merrily we welcome the year." One of the main speakers included the leader of the Chicano Migrant Workers Union, Caesar Chavez. In a large auditorium, on Fisherman's Wharf, having read her book *The Price of My Soul*, I was in the very large audience to see Bernadette Devlin presented with the Freedom of the City of San Francisco by Mayor Alioto.

My arrival in California in November 1968 was in the passenger seat of a truck driving a load of vegetables to Los Angeles from

Utah. As I was totally exhausted after the arduous journey when we arrived in the Los Angeles Fruit Market, I had to try and work out the monkey puzzle of survival just like all the other newcomers to California had to do, from the wagon trains and ever since. A song by The Band, penned by Robbie Robertson and popular at the time, summed up exactly how I felt: "I pulled in to Nazareth/I was feeling about half past dead/I just needed a place /where I can lay my head."

Another line from Country Joe McDonald expressed a dilemma with which I became familiar, "Standing on the LA Freeway rain water in my boots,/standing on the LA Freeway feeling kind of destitute."

In Santa Monica I secured a bus boy job with tips in the coffee shop in the Miramar Hotel. The tips were an invaluable asset for survival in the fiercely competitive world of Los Angeles, city of the Angels; but few if any of the angels that I met had their wings intact. Most were angels with broken wings. Venice Beach with the lively mix of the Sixties generation has many happy memories. After a small degree of research I visited frequently Shrine Lake, a park in Pacific Palisades on the coast founded by Paramanhsa Yogananda, an Indian Yogi mystic. The park contained a shoot from the Bodhi Tree under which Buddha meditated. The early morning visits were sometimes paid for by irregularly slipping over the fence. The ease and grace of the swans gliding at their own pace, untroubled by the mayhem of the world, were a source of great peace of mind when the morning sunlight was reflected in the rippling water. The peace park at Shrine Lake also contained some of the ashes of Mahatma Ghandi. I found a rare tranquillity when I visited Shrine Lake. In the wooden summer-house overlooking the lake was the inscription, "Be still and know that God is with you."

Another small enclave for an alternative to city madness was McArthur Park, visited by many troubled lives with the famous song named after it – so many people caught in the tangled web of friendships and difficult relationships. The Beatles were right: "There's a fog upon LA and our friends have lost their way./They'll be over soon they said/Now they have lost themselves instead." The engulfing swamp prompted an idea similar to the way a friend of mine was also thinking. Early in the New Year we had driven up to San Francisco in his truck.

In 1969 John Steinbeck died. I read his obituary by the Assistant Editor of the *Monterey Herald*, Joe Costelloe, when I was passing through Monterey. As I chatted to him he said "As one of young years you might find it embarrassing to hear a newspaper man talk frankly." Mr Costelloe pointed me in the direction of a man called Sparky who (as he told me himself) was a character in the Steinbeck novel *The Log of the Sea of Cortez*. Sparky's favourite Steinbeck book, the one which he thought was his best, was *Tortilla Flats*. My own preference would be *East of Eden*. Most of the books by John Steinbeck I saw on display behind glass in a restaurant that was the site of the old flophouse adjacent to Cannery Row, as I sipped an Irish coffee. As one Nobel laureate died in 1969, another was elevated: Samuel Beckett. Armstrong and Jones landed on the moon 21 July, 1969. In Candlestick Park the Beatles played together for the last time. In upstate New York, Woodstock took place.

It was like – as we thought in our innocence – the beginning of something which was not going to end, a carousel which would only gain momentum until it included the world and all its dominions. Little did we know that it would end so abruptly. The resting place for the Sixties was in all probability the Rolling Stones' farewell concert to their American fans at Altamont

Speedway on 6 December, 1969. I was in a prominent front-tier position. As The Rolling Stones hit into the ominous "Sympathy for the Devil," tragedy struck in the midst of the surging crowd of 300,000. The Hells Angels were acting as security at a dangerous flash-point; there was a violent fracas, and a man was dead.

A disenchanted Sixties warrior walked beside me, his long hair clinging in despondency, as we made for our separate directions. He enquired, "You got a cigarette?"

"I have two," I replied, "I'll give you one."

"I like your style," he chirped gratefully. If you have it you never lose it.

A MAN WITH A HAT

I FIRST saw it in Clerys of O'Connell Street, hanging on display in the hat department – a lonely sight in a way, only a shadow of its true self without a suitable owner of distinction to bring out the full surge of its potential.

Its smart, sharp brim suggested it would suit a man who had to make quick decisions – or perhaps know how to get out of trouble as quickly as possible. The two-inch band which marked its circumference looked like a kind of intellectual seat-belt that would allow its proud owner to be able to think about anything he wished in mental safety and comfort.

Then I noted the careful indentation at its crown with the two side creases between its centre point. The contemplative forest-green colour seemed perfect for a man like me who daily has to navigate his head and his life around many problems. I bought it.

Since then the hat has had a great assortment of interesting experiences. It could tell many stories about survival, mishaps, threatened loss of life. It could testify how freely dollars can disappear in a town such as Las Vegas, like water from a free-flowing tap, disappearing down the sink of free enterprise. It could give evidence that in the taxi to the airport, with only $10 to spare, you realise how lucky you are to be getting out of that town alive.

Fisherman's Wharf

The hat could smile knowingly, if it was capable of smiling. It has spent a restless night wandering around Fisherman's Wharf in San

Francisco, searching for solace until the dawn broke over San Francisco Bay. It has escorted me like a loyal Labrador friend on the eerie journey through the desolation and deep loneliness of foreign city streets. It rode a streetcar in New Orleans and had its photograph snapped outside the local jailhouse with its proud owner beaming a smile of freedom and flashing a peace sign against the backdrop of the Sheriff's department's police cars. It has flown over Phoenix, Arizona: Atlanta, Georgia: Houston, Texas and walked in the rush hour through the busy hustle bustle of Manhattan.

Nearer home, it has survived comments from passers-by in the streets of Dublin, from "Nice hat," "That's a cool hat," "Hiya cobber, you from Australia?" to "John Wayne – I like your hat," and "Are you Clint Eastwood?"

I felt like saying, "I'm more like Jesse James," but silence is sometimes the perfect loud retort to ignorance.

The hat has, I confess, survived many weekends of excess in the pubs. Temple Bar. It wants a peaceful life, but nothing is certain, and I believe gales are forecast and even war is on the horizon.

It has been unknowingly the closest witness to my most private thoughts and deepest wishes, a worthy ally of hopes, fears, dreams and aspirations. If it was called as a witness in a court case it could make a very eloquent character witness.

"Only some people can get away with wearing a hat – fair play to you," was a regular remark. Does this suggest that hat-wearers are a breed apart? Would it be possible to form a be-hatted community of latter-day musketeers who would scorn all acquiescence to the predictable and obvious whims of fashion and commerce? A kind of mad-hatter's tea party – ultimately a celebration of sanity by keeping a small space for people's right to be different?

Free thinker

Is headgear a fair guide to its owner's cast of mind? Is there a free thinker under the beret of a Frenchman? Is it a sign that he is not a Le Pen voter? Is every Stetson wearer a George Bush supporter, a kind of republican rodeo fan? Is the chap with the bowler, the pin-striped suit and the briefcase sitting on the Tube reading the *Daily Telegraph* on his way to work in a stockbroker's office in the City? Is he an arch-conservative who grows jingoistic after a few gins? Does he wax lyrical and sentimental when he recalls in the cricket club the great days of Margaret Thatcher?

The beret, the Stetson and the bowler, like the flags on a ship they denote identity and nationality. But sometimes they may also be a decoy, saying one thing but meaning something else, a mis-chievous ploy to keep secrets well hidden. A hat can be a poker player's friend, after all, keeping his eyes under cover. When he is ready to show his hand, then, like a painful and unwelcome crick in the neck, it suddenly hits you that you've been cleaned out by the guy with the hat.

Closing time

Anyway, I've now rejoined the ranks of the bare-headed. Here's how it happened. In a dimly lit basement in the early hours, just about closing time, I was sitting on my own. So was she. She was all of 22 years of age, with lips like Brigitte Bardot, a fringe like Liza Minelli and a heavy spray of lacquer in her hair. She chirped like a happy sparrow: "Can I try on your hat?"

"I'll make you a present of it," I offered in the spirit of goodwill and generosity, as she tried it on.

"No. I can't take it," she replied.

But I insisted – for at that moment, the hat seemed filled with the residue of all my worries. Give it away to the young lady with the lacquer in her hair and I could wave them goodbye.

Her face brightened up with a chandelier smile as she walked out into the night to get a taxi home, wearing my hat. So, I had another drink from the friendly barman and I thought to myself: if she only knew what that hat and I had been through.

PLACES I'VE LIVED IN

WHERE I LIVE suits me. It is a flat, at least people used to call the place in which they lived a "flat" if it was rented accommodation. Nowadays the domicile rented cave is christened by the inglorious plumage of "apartment." The modern nest of comfortable habitation is pronounced by floral rolling r's, suitably accentuated are the two strong "a" vowels to make it sound like "ahpurtment." Whether the rent or the mortgage is being paid on the ahpurtment is another story, or whether there is any food in the fridge of the ahpurtment is not my business. But Newspeak pronounces it "ahpurtment."

But like everywhere else I have lived it has something to offer as it helps to prolong my life. The living room, with a kitchen snugly inbuilt, and a welcome fireplace lends an aspect of cosiness and accessibility. A regular bad habit are sheets of A4 paper littering the living room, just like losing betting slips in any self-respecting bookie's office, literary clues to my progress as a gent with an inky story to tell.

A globe balances on a semi-circle curved stand on a desk. Very often fresh flowers in water with healthy brimming shoots are a regular part of the landscape, just like a farewell kiss I've been saving up to all the past dives that I've lived in. The postal code of this part of the city is Dublin 8, you could say "Dublin Ate You Alive." But not true as I've been living here just over three years and so far I've survived quite well on a modest budget.

There are four windows, one in the living room, one in a small hallway and two in the bedroom. One window opens up into what is a real gift – a balcony. While I have not become a farmer with wellingtons and a tractor, this time last year I planted a generous helping of bulbs in moderate sized red earthenware pots. When the shoots appeared, it was for me like the dawning of creation on the first day of the planet Earth. Now, in spite of all my worst fears about myself, I am quite likely to suffer from green fingers.

In the living room hangs pride of place a painting by a friend, a portrait of a young woman. The eyes of the woman look in the right-hand direction, like she feels that she is almost too sensitive to bear public gaze. But such nobility in the posture of her head thus tilted at an angle, like she knows unassumingly how priceless is her great dignity, protected by her shyness.

During my travels, members of my family were only fleeting faces with voices which telephoned floated images onto my mind. Now they are neatly arranged in a line of photographs on the mantlepiece: two of my nieces, now in the full bloom of mother-hood, in bathing suits on the beach, their captivating smiles revealing – even to viewers who are unknown to them – happy days with the hospitality air-hostess experience beaming from their friendly well-disposed good looks. A confirmation photograph of my younger sister with my mother, taken late 1950s. Visible in the photograph, my sister Eileen's eyes with a gentle look of girlhood, spiritual tenderness, yet such a defiant chin with a serious purpose. My mother's contrasting expression of world experience, but with a mother's joy in hope for future promise. A photograph of a family shop on The Diamond in Clones, Co Monaghan. There, my grandfather, although blind, earned a living – as did my Aunt Eileen – and my brothers and my sisters and I helped out on school holidays, especially on the great day of the Ulster football final. It contains so many memories of past but not forgotten happy days. In a photograph of my nephew's wedding, he looking relaxed and happy with his serene bride and proud father and mother, with the solidarity of my two nephews – brotherly loyalty and support.

The bedroom and bathroom have just been painted with a finish of mint colour. This week it is the turn of the living room and hallway, a freshening of complexion to enliven the pallor of three years of absent paint. Some – perhaps light green – tiles in the kitchen to replace the lino, and similarly in the bathroom, no Kelly-green, more a DUCK EGG green!

A recent acquisition, a CD holder with a generous spaciousness, invites – indeed begs – its space to be neatly filled, and prevent the mild chaos of visible CDs. The bookcase in the living room contains the fairly lively recent poetry acquisitions: Collected Mahon, Selected Longley, Collected Lawrence Durrell, John Berryman and William Carlos Williams. But how do I get hold of the out-of-print selected poems of Padraic Fiacc?

On a small table stands a cactus plant from Phoenix, Arizona, with eight shoots of leaves reaching for the walls and ceiling. Two glass vases, like oversized lemonade glasses, sit on the mantlepiece, my only concession to disingenuous plant-life: in each glass a shoot of blackberries, cherries and pussywillows weighted in the resting place by some oversized pebbles and small stones and some seaweed, submerged in water collected on a Sunday afternoon recently on the seashore in Dun Laoghaire.

Two recently acquired blue lampshades make a welcome contrast to the lonely spectacle and desolation of naked light-bulbs. The net curtains rejuvenated from the laundry on Patrick Street – with a wooden curtain rail and the slightly low-hanging green rose-patterned drapes on this January, early morning – give a comfortable sealed-in security.

Our cities and towns these days, like howling wolves in the Yukon, seem to possess a blood-curdling cry for mayhem and destruction. This is Dublin South Central of the nation's capital, but side-by-side with the residue of poverty, homelessness, drugs and drink, there is also a nobility and inspiration.

In ways this is the most disadvantaged part of any town or city in the country. A majority of the low-income groupings comprise the homeless and marginalised. They are tightly squeezed by the cruel fist of the poverty trap. That is the economic noose which cleverly betrayed them, by not allowing them safe distance from debt, deprivation, dependencies on alcohol and drugs, and gambling, which results in the humiliation of begging, muggings and robbery with violence.

"We are the poor of Canterbury, living a half-living." This is how TS Eliot described the poor of Canterbury in *Murder in the Cathedral*. For the poor of Dublin, the same truth obtains, as the ever-mounting waves of deprivation make the shore-line of safe ground less visible, and very often they flounder and drown tragically. If the sad waltz of the marginalised is to be redressed and be made less unhappy – the high pressure point of their dilemmas must be highlighted: accommodation, medical services, self-help and educational resources are a high priority. The culture of disenfranchisement needs research at medical school level, in nursing schools and in university social work departments.

Early one morning last year, looking through the hallway window which faces the busy doctor's surgery across the street, I saw a tall young lanky male who appeared half crazed. He grabbed a mother's baby infant from its buggy – then hurriedly disappeared, babe in arms, down a laneway. The highly terrified and panic-stricken mother was understandably aghast and frozen with shock, and unhinged from the roots of her being. I quickly got the number of nearby Kevin Street Garda Station from the directory – and a Ban Garda and a Guard arrived in a squad car with professional promptness. Happily the infant was returned a short time later, but what an ordeal of horror and trauma for the mother! This was just one of the hidden daily dramas and heartbreaks secluded quietly in the poorer alcoves of the land of the Celtic Tiger.

On the arrival in Reykjavik Iceland, myself and my Australian buddy checked into the cheapest accommodation, the Salvation Anny, which was home also for the local dispossessed – Reykjavik gentry living on welfare. So we felt completely at home bonding with people like ourselves who had absolutely nothing in the way of collateral.

The room we shared certainly had an aura of bleak penury hovering like a ghost of destitution about the place, other inmates of this space of enforced monasticism with vow of poverty high on its list of priorities. A souvenir to posterity was carved by a previous tenant of this abode of destitution on the inside of the wardrobe door the immortal words carved with a penknife "fed up, fucked up and far from home."

Hitch-hiking in Spain, studying on the roadside outside Alicante I got a lift from a very special person. He became my very good friend. He did not speak a word of English. He only spoke Arabic, as he was from Moroc (as he called it). Neither did I speak any of the Moroc lingo. He pulled up on the roadway at my feet, just outside Alicante. He beamed a happy, grinning, moustachioed smile. He was small of build, with an almost dancing merriment of joy in his eyes. And what a gas we had on our journey through Andalucia, Murcia, ending up when he caught the ferry from Algecerus to Tangier. The small cream coloured Fiat took us over Sierra Nevada and the great rolling storm clouds of southern Spain. The cloud formations were mind blowing – all that floating, vaporous, ghost-like trails of glory heading for the Mediterranean ocean. The scenery was breathtaking, along the straight table-top sections of roadway. The pueblos of poverty, carved into the hillsides of the soul of Spain was to experience a bit of real greatness and beauty. When we arrived in Granada he was overjoyed because he was a short skip and jump home to Moroc. In Granada on our arrival he was only ready and fit after the long journey to disintegrate into sleep. Myself, I took myself off to a hotel bar and San Miguel Cervesa.

In Gibraltar, with the international travellers who were on the move around the world I made great friends. One memorable aspect of the morning stroll around the small courtyard of Toc-H founded by the venerable Baden Powell as this home from home was called, the memory of distinction were the amiable baboons who were on a morning walkabout in the foothills of Gibraltar. Mobile as they were from their more permanent home high up on the rocky peaks of the Rock of Gibraltar itself, the baboons at this time of the morning slumming it with the visiting tourists. I had visited them in their own native habitat high up on the rock summit at this high altitude one cheeky baboon was a little over friendly with an American tourist to express his over enthusiastic friendliness he jumped up on the back of this lady tourist, bit her, grabbed her handbag and made off up the hill.

In Las Palmas, Gran Canaria, with a borrowed sleeping bag while seriously bankrupt, financially shipwrecked and materially beached far from home and roofless, I made the ultimate usage of the semi-rock surface protected by a wall barrier from the sea breeze a Playa de Ingles adjacent to the Parca Santa Catalina. On the nearby docks of the fishing marina another night refuge was the captain's roomy sleeping quarters. This terminated with a swift exit in early daylight with a diligent crew member acting as security in swift pursuit. This was January 1967, I had just reached my twentieth birthday.

My friend, Steve, from Durban, South Africa, was also stranded and in the same predicament as myself. He had just seen too much of the world and at that stage just wanted to see home again. In the course of his travels he had learned six languages and, oh what stories he had to tell! Each morning we met up in the same place under a particular tree in Parca Santa Catalina and plotted how, without money, we could get the hell out of Las Palmas. I don't know what happened to Steve as this happened just over thirty-seven years ago. I got a job as a steward on a German tanker the "Gunter Ross" based in Hamburg. We travelled across the Atlantic, 150 miles up the Orinoco river in Venezuela to the Amazon basin and the village of Carapito to refuel and pick up a cargo of oil for America.

The machine guns of the military which protected the valuable black, liquid gold, came as a surprise. I thought maybe if I got ashore I could get to Bolivia and look up Che Guevara. To the uninitiated, the Amazon jungle, alone and unprotected in the middle of the night, is really not the place to be. The sound of the insect orchestra, of loud crazy weird noises and deafening sounds, is frightening, but there was also the distinct possibility of snake bites. That is of course unless you are a local breed of monkey living in the trees, or a local normal friendly ordinary and neighbourly panther, just ambling around, out for an evening stroll. But for me it was not really the place to be, because a safe and sound good night's sleep was not really on the cards. So I returned to my bunk on the ship, even if it was filled with cabin fever.

I jumped ship in Newhaven, Connecticut, February 1967 and hitch-hiked into the deep southern states, staying a while to receive the hospitality of a friend's parents in Jackson, Mississippi.

Hitch-hiking towards the Gulf of Mexico and New Orleans – in Northern Mississippi I met Tom, who lived with his mother and young sister and brother. He gave me a lift in the late afternoon. He could have been driving a black Buick or whatever, not exactly in mint condition. But he was one talkative, half over-talkative, the other half just friendly and well disposed towards strangers like myself, who seemed very well disposed towards him, and the world generally, which I definitely was. Tom did not make the frame for the Navy – the test and all. His wonderful mother, that evening, in a poor Mississippi household told me that the commanding officer in the navy drove Tom home when he failed his test. Driving around in early nightfall Tom drove to the gates of Graceland (Elvis Presley's mansion home) and he said as we were parked directly in front of the gate, he said very excitedly, "Now John, you go up to that security guard there, you tell him you've come all the way from Dublin, Ireland to meet the king of rock 'n roll. Now John, you go on – you go tell him – you tell him you've come all the way from Ireland to meet the king of rock 'n roll." And after spending approximately two seconds thinking about it – I declined the opportunity.

When, some years later, on a bleak rainy Dublin evening on the corner of Bachelors Walk, I read the headline, "The King of Rock 'n Roll was Dead," I thought back to the gates of Graceland and how close I might have been to meeting him. But who knows, maybe we would just have led each other further astray, if that were possible!

I have had a number of memorable – shall we call them euphemistically "residencies": Reykjevik, Iceland, a dim dingy attic in the heart of a dark arctic winter, meals for three in this box-room cooked on a Primus stove – and trying to write poetry by candlelight – but oh what happy days! A ramshackle kitchen and bedroom, north of Wilshire Boulevard in Santa Monica, circa Christmas 1968. The poor landlord, who continually called for the rent, without success. Eventually I felt sorry for him and his dilemma, he struck a deep chord with the gentleman in me. So I took the honourable course of action, before the poor harassed and distraught man had a heart attack – or alternatively he might just call the cops. So I vacated the apartment, and made him a happy man, even if not a wealthy one.

On the beach in Las Palomas, Gran Canaria, January 1967, with my companions from London and Yorkshire, we made a makeshift "residence" – branches and palm leaves and oddments of wood that we could salvage. The tourists on vacation invariably left their picnics behind in the evening. We beach-combers were then efficiently on the move. The wind, after a time, blowing in from the Atlantic, became excessive, so we blew it too. This staging post was rent free, which was a big help because everybody in the group was more or less broke.

For the wanderer, sometimes nature and the smile of the angels can be a marvellous host and benefactor, with haystacks, barns, cushioned seats of trains not going anywhere, and public parks. Outside Memphis, Tennessee, in an automobile wreckers' yard was like a night in the Hilton with highly-sprung back-seat cushions, easy on the spine, and Southern night temperature, was just about perfect. A friendly desk sergeant in a conservative English town provided beds for me and my pal in his comfortable cell. Intrigued, he wondered of us, half-dazed by lack of sleep on our travels, where we were headed next.

The freight train, with many empty wagons resting in the stockyards of Portland, Oregon, falling asleep and happily heading for the Canadian border, the jolting halt into wakefulness as the front wagons of the train snaked forward to Canada, my humble bedroom – that is, the wagon I was in – was made redundant from the other sections of the train and left behind.

The Bay area of San Francisco 1969, adjacent to Sausalito, which is located in Marin County not too far from the Golden Gate

Bridge. In a marina for seagoing craft of many types from catamarans to yachts, the fishing boats and motor boats, my friend Lenny from New York had his own unique creation. About a mile out in the bay there rested majestically a boat he had built himself, shaped like a Roman galley ship. At the end of a night with friends, with a few drinks taken, the obstacle course was indeed perilous and risky, to row in a small rowing boat out to the floating sleeping quarters in the bay. So if the currents of alcohol as well as seawater were too choppy, it was a tension and drama-filled journey. But if the Gods of Bacchus and Neptune were smiling favourably, at the journey's end was the prospect of a blissful night's sleep with gentle waves lapping rhythmically against the boat's woodwork.

Encinitas, Southern California, close to an ashram of followers of the Indian mystic Paramanhansa Yogananda. A seeker who was an ex-Mormon from Utah offered me sleeping-bag space in his fine tent. The next morning I awoke within a short distance of a small orchard of gleaming yellow-skinned grapefruits reflected in the sunlight. A Hari Krishna monk on the nearby beach waxed lyrical about the joy of a Swami master. Mr McCrae was right, "Oh what a beautiful morning!"

A snooze I can recall with a sweet sense of nostalgia – hitchhiking across Canada from Toronto to the Rocky Mountains. I got a lift with a trucker from Texas, crossing the prairies of Saskatawan. The Texas drawl, "idear" instead of "idea," and all the folksy at-home southern hospitality. As the endless flatness of the prairies monotonously rolled by on the trans-Canadian highway – I was ensconced in the land of nod in the driver's bunk-bed at the rear of the cab – catching forty winks.

On a fishing marina of Victoria, Vancouver Island, hospitality was offered and accepted from the captain of a salmon run boat, and given with great courtesy. So I fell asleep thinking of home, friends and family, nearly half a world away, just on the cusp of my twenty-second birthday.

We are descended from killer apes, scientists inform us, and oh how primitive we can behave. But in our being is there somewhere a small seed of vision expanding which does, as is the way with plants and growing things, break ground? Just like the plants on my balcony. A flower we are waiting on to bloom, to make us smile in the face of misfortune, so also happy endings are part of life. It occurs to my lie-detector of survival, which Ernest Hemingway called "His shit shock proof detector," which we are all endowed with compliments of the Creator.

The following truth if some of the sad endings, being unhappily played out all around us, are in some way dictated by the absence of vision, political or otherwise. So also some situations which young people are invited, or rather coerced, by shallow TV and its willing accomplice of worse advertising for some alleged classic brand of alcohol will give you, free of charge, your stud papers to perform with the female as opaque as the drink you are skulled on. So you can both get out of your minds together! And unhappily destroy each other, all thanks to the rotten poison which cleverly tricked both of you into not knowing what you were doing. So regrettably leaving no forward notice on the bottle you were drinking from to tell you that your lovely drinking partner is pregnant. A lick of my own wit, the one about the beautiful Indian Princess who got pregnant by the American GI, she said, "Who's sari now?" Ultimately, I do not think youth invited the above charade and gobbledygook into their lives, so not having invited it in, I hope they shovel it out as quickly as possible.

JOHN McNAMEE BY HIMSELF

I HAVE WORKED at many and various jobs in Ireland, England, Canada and America. The jobs have included labourer in Camden Town; dishwasher; barman; cleaner; kitchen porter; factory worker in a fish factory in Grindavik, Iceland; deckhand on a trawler on the Icelandic National Fleet; bus boy in Santa Monica, California; kitchen help in San Francisco; Aid in a half way house in Victoria, Vancouver Island; steward on a German tanker; pearl diver (otherwise known as dishwasher), Las Palmas Gran Canaria; temporary Clerical Officer, Rates Department, Dublin County Council, Parnell Square; cleaner, Mater Hospital, Dublin; Path Lab Porter, Nottingham General Hospital; factory hand, Birds Eye Food, Grimsby; machinist in Chivers Hartley Foods, Peterborough, Lincs. Since January 1998 I have been presenter/organiser of the popular Out to Lunch Poetry Readings, held on alternate Fridays, 1.15pm to 2.00pm in the Bank of Ireland Arts Centre, Foster Place, Dublin 2.

Writing for me is very often the raindrop of a thought falling onto the leaf of a blank page. A mighty atom which explodes from the mind and soul, to move in the undergrowth, the submarine and unconscious seeking like a human fish particles of plankton called truth. If the truth of the fish is something to eat to stay alive, then the truth for a writer is whatever morsels of the human character or whatever beauty of the human personality he can shape into a form with an edge and a cut of dignity and compassion which will make him continue.

Ultimately, the shape will in many ways be invisible, a sketchy haze of floating cloud on a hillside. So then with the soulful engine of creativity a person is seen collecting sticks – on a closer look it is the stooped fragile figure of an elderly lady with a black woollen shawl and floral dress a scarf tied tightly around her neck to keep in the heat. She wears a black gansey to keep out the winter chill. It is just prior to the potato famine in Ireland a small stone cottage is visible at the bottom of the hill with smoke coming from the chimney a cock can be heard crowing to the new day and the cattle are lowing. So it is over 175 years ago the place may change and the time but the creative process which lights up the world and makes it visible does not. It is the lantern in the human soul from which all writing and all art originates.

In cities, including Dublin, I have seen the despressed spirits in the unwell. A bubbling volcano of human sorrow. It is obvious all is not well and many are very unwell. Yet the dawn breaks every day on cities all over the world and there is hope. From Baghdad to Washington, Dublin, London, Paris and Shanghai. In spite of the newspapers headlines and the 6.00pm news there is a silk purse in the richness of people, God-given which cannot be bought at any price either on Wall Street or at an art auction. The priceless miracle of life even with all the heartbreak, love can achieve anything most of all happiness for people.

Pet hate words are "Actually," "In Fact," "Unfortunately," "not available," "at a meeting," "out of the country," answering machines with a hollow centred mantra "I'm either away from my desk," "on the phone," or "out of the office."

Favourite film *Rocco and His Brothers*, director Visconti – reason tells the truth about how horrible poverty really is, in Italy or anywhere else.

Favourite play *Waiting for Godot* by Sam Beckett – reason something about a man when all he has is the desolation of a park bench on a bleak winter twilight. "A poetic non materialist spiritual truth."

Favourite poem "The Fool" by Padraig Pearse which describes

beautifully what fools most of us really are.

Favourite poet Patrick Kavanagh "The Paddiad" – reason because it describes all the Paddies in the one Irishman.

Favourite Irish person Sonia O'Sullivan – reason she never gives up.

Least favourite person myself when I have neither the money for a cigarette, a drink or the rent.

Favourite song "The Hobo's Lullaby" – reason a good song is fitting homage to greatness.

Favourite female singer Billie Holliday.

Favourite song "Good Morning Heartache" – reason sometimes love is just too good to last and you get a wake-up call that you got too comfortable and you were not trying hard enough and that's your own business.

Favourite rock 'n roll band The Band and Robbie Robertson.

Favourite song "The Shape I'm in" – reason I have lived the words.

Favourite painting The Umbrellas by Renoir – reason sometimes life is all about trying to stay out of the rain.

Favourite piece of music Aida "The March of the Egyptians" by Verdi – reason because it understands deeply the burden of people and lifts a huge weight.

Hopes for the future include a better life for people with dignity and style and without opulent vulgarity.

Most impressive person I ever met Louis Armstrong – reason because he gave so much of himself.

Best political speech I have ever heard Senator Robert Kennedy Jr, Presidential campaign, Kennedy Square, Detroit, May 1968 – reason he genuinely cared about people.

Previous books by John McNamee

Flight (Poems)
Sparrow Press, National Poetry Society, London, 1977

Trawling off Iceland
Zoot Publications, Dublin, 1978

The Worm in the Heart
Merlin Publications, Dublin, 1984

Ascendant Mood (Poems)
Weaver Publications, Dublin, 1987

New and Selected Poems
Weaver Publications, Dublin, 1990

Poetry Reading (Cassette)
Dublin, 1989

The Trophy and New Writings
Weaver Publications, Dublin, 1992

Editor, *Out to Lunch: Poets from Dublin's Lunchtime Readings Series*
Bank of Ireland Arts Centre, Dublin, 2002

Out to Lunch (CD – Poetry reading)
Dublin, 2003

Co-wrote *Kangaroo Rats* (Play)
Produced in the Dublin Fringe Theatre Festival, 1995